POCKET

HAMBURG

TOP SIGHTS · LOCAL EXPERIENCES

D0877067

ANTHONY HAM

Contents

Plan Your Trip

St Michaelis Kirche (p58)
JOAQUIN OSSORIO CASTILLO/SHUTTERSTOCK ©

Welcome to Hamburg

Hamburg is one of the coolest cities on earth. A maritime spirit infuses the entire city, bequeathing its diverse neighbourhoods astonishing culinary, architectural and musical excellence and variety. To put it another way, it's impossible to come to Hamburg and not have a really good time.

Hamburg harbour

Top Sights

JANIS MALECKIS/SHUTTERSTOCK ©

Elbphilharmonie
An architectural icon, with world-class music. **p86**

FOTO-SELECT/SHUTTERSTOCK ©

Rathaus
Hamburg's grandest medieval building. **p42**

Hamburger Kunsthalle

Outstanding art spanning the ages. **p40**

CLAUDIO DIVIZIA/SHUTTERSTOCK ©

LEFT: CLAUDIO DIVIZIA/SHUTTERSTOCK ©
RIGHT: FRANK GAERTNER/SHUTTERSTOCK ©

Mahnmal St-Nikolai

Haunting monument with
extraordinary views. **p38**

Fischmarkt

Hamburg's Sunday-morning
happy hour. **p102**

St Michaelis Kirche

Baroque city landmark with views. **p58**

Internationales Maritimes Museum

Maritime excellence in HafenCity. **p88**

LEFT: SURATH SRIGAMA/SHUTTERSTOCK ©
RIGHT: OHO7/BILDAGENTUR-ONLINE/ALAMY ©

RITU MANOJ JETHANI/SHUTTERSTOCK ©

Miniatur Wunderland

Europe in miniature. **p90**

Eating

Virtually every part of Hamburg has good dining options, ranging from humble to fine. Unsurprisingly, seafood is a favourite in this port city, with everything from traditional regional specialities to sushi on offer. You'll also find a truly global variety of foods reflecting this city's international links and traditions, but don't neglect the widely available local specialities.

Local Specialities

On paper, Germany's (and Hamburg's) best-known specialities appear deceptively simple: *wurst*, *brot*, *kartoffeln* and *sauerkraut* (sausage, bread, potatoes and pickled cabbage).

Labskaus

If there's one Hamburg or northern German dish that Hamburgers love more than any other, it's *labskaus*. The constituent ingredients are potato, cured beef, herrings and beetroot (the latter gives it the rather lurid colour that distinguishes true *labskaus*) and although it's usually called a stew, 'mash' would be more accurate. It's usually served topped with an egg.

Fischbrötchen

Finding the perfect *fischbrötchen* (fish roll or fish sandwich; pictured) is something of a Hamburg obsession, at once lunchtime snack or late-night comfort food for those on the way home from a big night out. It's a very simple dish, with a piece of pickled herring (sometimes salted, sometimes sweet) served in a small roll, often with a token piece of lettuce.

Best Restaurants

Das Dorf German specialities, cooked to perfection in St Georg. (p79)

Deichgraf Local specialities in a gorgeous Hamburg street. (p51)

Die Bank One of Hamburg's most prestigious restaurants. (p67)

AGE FOTOSTOCK/ALAMY ©

Alt Hamburger Aalspeicher Home cooking in a down-home setting. (p45)

Altes Mädchen Part of Hamburg's new-wave dining scene. (p131)

Fischbrötchenbude Brücke 10 Pickled herring in a roll in Hamburg – tick! (p111)

Best Labskaus

Das Dorf Try their *labskaus* with their homemade bread – two German passions in one. (p79)

Laufauf No-frills restaurant with terrific, hearty *labskaus*. (p45)

Deichgraf Upmarket restaurant with large and small *labskaus* offerings. (p51)

Old Commercial Room Longstanding *labskaus* classic next to St Michaelis Kirche. (p65)

Best Fischbrötchen

Fischbrötchenbude Brücke 10 Our pick for the best *fischbrötchen*, down by the port. (p111)

Atlantik Fisch Twenty different types and many people's prize for the best in town. (p132)

Kleine Haie Grosse Fische Late-night fish sandwiches as comfort food in the heart of Reeperbahn's party zone. (p105)

Drinking & Nightlife

Hamburg's nightlife is legendary, and rightly so. Elite cocktail bars, nonstop nightclubs and world-class DJs are all part of a mix that rocks and rolls with energy and innovation. Hamburg is renowned for its electro-punk sound, which started in the 1980s and has evolved and morphed endlessly. Clubkombinat (www.clubkombinat.de) has club listings.

Bars & Pubs

The mainstay of Hamburg's drinking culture, this catch-all category includes the rough-and-tumble neighbourhood pubs of St Pauli and the quietly sophisticated bars of Altona. Most open around 5pm during the week, earlier on weekends, and stay open until the last customer staggers out the door.

When it comes to city beaches, you have to salute Hamburgers for their can-do spirit. Undeterred by their renowned *Schmuddelwetter* (drizzly weather), they've built little sandy enclaves on the banks of the Elbe, where they can enjoy a beer on the sand.

Brewery Bars

Old-style beer cellars or other traditional drinking houses where the beer used to be (and sometimes still is) brewed on the premises. Craft beers are pushing their way into this scene.

Nightclubs

Don't even think of visiting a Hamburg nightclub before midnight. Some don't even get going until after 2am. Some Hamburg nightclubs have cover charges, and those that don't play catch-up with expensive drinks.

Best Nightlife

Le Lion Hamburg's most exclusive cocktail bar and home of the gin basil smash – as good as it sounds. (p53)

Molotow We *love* this legendary Reeperbahn nightclub. (p115)

Bar Hamburg Dress your best for this smooth-as-silk cocktail bar. (p81)

Zum Silbersack Everything and everyone you'd want in a St Pauli bar. (p105)

Bacaro Wine Bar Slick and contemporary St Georg wine bar. (p80)

CCLPHOTOGRAPHY/SHUTTERSTOCK ©

Best Cocktail Bars

Le Lion The king of Hamburg cocktail bars, in Altstadt. (p53)

Bar Hamburg Beloved by celebrity A-listers in St Georg. (p81)

Clouds Bar Rooftop cocktails high above Reeperbahn. (p114)

Katze Hamburg's best caipirinhas over in Altona. (p133)

Best Brewery Bars & Craft Beers

Gröninger Privatbrauerei Try the home brew straight from the barrel in the historic cellar. (p45)

Biergarten Speersort Bavarian beer garden in the finest tradition of southern Germany. (p53)

Kyti Voo Craft beers dominate the drinks list in this terrific St Georg bar. (p82)

Best Neighbourhood Bars

Zum Silbersack Classic St Pauli pub that draws everyone in Hamburg. (p105)

Zur Ritze Eclectic Reeperbahn bar, at once risqué and mainstream with an occasional celebrity. (p114)

Bacaro Wine Bar Classy St Georg wine bar and symbol of the new stylish Hamburg. (p80)

Golden Pudel Club St Pauli alternative icon with music in its soul. (p114)

Komet Musik Bar Vinyl records, its very own drink, and a loyal crowd – classic St Pauli. (p115)

Aurel Inviting Altona bar with a long drinks list and great music. (pictured; p125)

Best Nightclubs

Molotow Epic Reeperbahn nightclub that never slows down. (p115)

Golden Cut Club High-end weekend-only club in St Georg. (p81)

Nachtasyl Longstanding city-centre nightspot whose popularity never wanes. (p54)

Moondoo Draws some of the best DJs in Germany and Europe. (p117)

Shopping

Hamburg's shopping may not rival its nightlife in profile, but there are numerous interesting finds – from mainstream to offbeat – as you explore the city. As a general rule, shopping possibilities reflect the neighbourhoods they inhabit – Neustadt and Altstadt are refined and upmarket, while St Pauli, Altona and St Georg have more boutiques and artsy corner shops.

Best by Neighbourhood

Altstadt Large department stores and bookstores, but a few smaller boutiques. (pictured; p54)

Neustadt Hamburg's shopping central with designer brands everywhere. (p69)

St Georg Little boutiques and quirky shops along Lange Reihe. (p83)

St Pauli & Reeperbahn Grungy and artsy if you know where to look. (p121)

Altona & Elbmeile Boutiques, fashion and homewares. (p135)

Best Boutiques & Markets

Mutterland The perfect German deli for gifts, picnics or a naughty sweet treat. (p70)

Flohschanze Excellent Saturday flea market in Karolinenviertel. (p121)

Koppel 66 Numerous stores and workshops selling arts and crafts under one roof. (p75)

Atelier Nigoh Beautiful little backstreet store, often with Hamburg-themed artworks. (p125)

Apropos the Concept Store International designer accessories displayed like works of art. (p71)

Fischmarkt Sunday-morning fish market with irresistible energy. (p102)

Best Souvenirs

Atelier Nigoh Gorgeous artworks with a Hamburg theme in St Pauli. (p125)

Kaufhaus Hamburg Fun Hamburg-themed gifts in St Georg. (p83)

Art of Hamburg Hamburg gifts with a focus on homewares. (p83)

Hamburger SV City Store Football shirts and souvenirs from Hamburger SV. (p45)

ALBERT PEGO/SHUTTERSTOCK ©

Best Homewares, Art & Design

Koppel 66 Hamburg's arts and crafts hub in St Georg. (p75)

Sleeping Dogs Concept store spanning vintage to Scandinavian style. (p54)

Wohnkultur 66 Danish work-of-art furnishings out in Altona. (p135)

Søstrene Grene Mainstream Scandinavian homewares and knick-knacks, in Altona. (p125)

Anne Zimmer Beautifully designed jewellery in a quiet corner of Neustadt. (p61)

Ars Japonica Tasteful Japanese prints and other perfectly formed items. (p121)

Best Food & Drink

Mutterland German delicatessen of the highest order, with most things perfectly packaged. (p70)

Tobias Strauch Weinkontor One of Hamburg's best wine shops, out in Neustadt's west. (p71)

Weinkauf St Georg German and other wines along Lange Reihe. (p83)

Best Clothes & Fashion

Neustadt Spend any time walking through this neighbourhood and you'll find Hamburg's best fashion shopping. (p69)

Apropos the Concept Store High-class designer accessories in this prestigious Neustadt address. (p71)

Crazy Jeans St Pauli fashions with attitude – is there any other kind? (p121)

Chapeau St Georg Hats, old and new, are all they sell here. (p83)

Museums & Galleries

Hamburg's cultural offering is astonishingly rich. Major art galleries, shadowed by smaller private galleries, share the city with important museums covering everything from an overview of Hamburg's history to emigration, maritime stories, the coffee trade and even some that zero in on Hamburg's stellar musical heritage.

Art Galleries

One Hamburg art gallery rises above all the rest: the Hamburger Kunsthalle (p40) is a world-class affair spanning the centuries from the Renaissance to contemporary times. Landmark names range from Klee to Caspar David Friedrich, and the architecture perfectly sets the stage – the stately surrounds of the early galleries take in medieval portraiture and the like, while the cube-like Galerie der Gegenwart takes a thoroughly modern slant on life, with David Hockney and his kind.

Museums

As a port city, Hamburg has always taken a broad-church approach to life, welcoming people and influences from across the globe. Its museums take a similar view. The city's maritime history is well looked after, from the maritime museum and a shipboard museum at Rickmer Rickmers (p110) to trade items such as chocolate, spices and coffee. There's also the world in miniature, plus small and quirky neighbourhood museums, while some would say that the Rote Flora cultural centre (p128) over in St Pauli is the essence of Hamburg's counterculture alter ego.

Musical Museums

Few cities can match Hamburg's musical pedigree, so it should come as no surprise that when the city was looking for an iconic architectural showpiece, it settled

BILDAGENTUR-ONLINE/JOKO/ALAMY ©

on a concert hall. The catalogue of classical music giants either from Hamburg or with a lifelong connection to the city is truly extraordinary: Carl Philipp Emanuel Bach (1714–88), Felix Mendelssohn (1809–47), Johannes Brahms (1833–97) and Gustav Mahler (1860–1911). Much later, a very different cast of musical geniuses – the Beatles – also left their mark on the city. Learn about it all at the Johannes Brahms Museum (p61) and Komponisten-Quartier (p61).

Best Art Galleries

Hamburger Kunsthalle Hamburg's premier art exhibition space, worth as much time as you can give it. (p40)

Museum für Kunst und Gewerbe Everything from furniture to porcelain with Japanese posters and pop art thrown in. (pictured; p77)

Deichtorhallen Stunning early-20th-century venue with temporary exhibitions. (p48)

Galerie Commeter Hamburg's oldest gallery, with a private collection spanning genres. (p48)

Galerie Herold Small private gallery focusing on northern German expressionist painters. (p63)

Best Museums

Internationales Maritimes Museum Expansive collection devoted to Hamburg's maritime past. (p88)

Johannes Brahms Museum Fascinating journey through the life of Hamburg's dearest musical son. (p61)

Mahnmal St-Nikolai Haunting exhibition on WWII's impact on Hamburg and elsewhere. (p38)

Speicherstadt Museum Hamburg's trading past in a fine old warehouse. (p93)

Museum für Hamburgische Geschichte Interactive Hamburg history for beginners. (p108)

Sankt Pauli Museum Mischievous neighbourhood museum in the best St Pauli tradition. (p105)

Architecture

Hamburg's city centre was all but destroyed during WWII, but a few pockets of old Hamburg survive. The city's churches showcase a range of architectural periods, but it's down by the waterfront that Hamburg's own architectural style shines. The dockland warehouses of Speicherstadt are quintessential Hamburg, while HafenCity has some dazzling contemporary structures.

Hamburg Gothic & Neo-Gothic

Thanks to WWII, there's not a whole lot that survives in Hamburg from the heyday of Gothic architecture, which arose in the 12th century and lasted until the 16th century. But its influence is still strong in the city, especially in the neo-Gothic gables and cornices of Speicherstadt.

Baroque Hamburg

Although little baroque architecture has survived in Hamburg, there are two splendid exceptions. The Rathaus (p42) is one of Germany's most beautiful, and is considered a masterpiece of the baroque or neo-Renaissance style. The other example is the St Michaelis Kirche (p58) – what you see today is a 1906 replica of the 18th-century original; the white-and-gold interior is considered classic baroque.

Modern Hamburg Architecture

The early 20th century was a time of great prosperity in Hamburg. The Hauptbahnhof (p141) was unveiled in 1906, when the stately homes of wealthy merchants began to appear around Binnenalster and Aussenalster.

In recent times, the city's architects have returned to traditional motifs or seagoing themes. The most obvious example is the Elbphilharmonie (p86), which evokes ocean waves through its extraordinary curved glass panels atop a traditional brick warehouse. The old docklands area known as HafenCity (p93) is fast becom-

DIZZY PHOTOS/SHUTTERSTOCK ©

ing an icon of contemporary architecture.

Best Gothic & Neo-Gothic Architecture

Krameramtswohnungen A row of tiny half-timbered houses from the 17th century. (p63)

Deichstrasse Gentrified, gabled houses in the Gothic style lining a cobblestone thoroughfare. (p45)

Johannes Brahms Museum Outpost of Gothic architecture out in the west of Neustadt with similar surrounding buildings. (p61)

Chilehaus Leading example of German expressionist architecture, with glazed bricks and gables. (p45)

Best Contemporary Architecture

Elbphilharmonie Stunning contemporary symbol of maritime Hamburg overlooking the port. (p86)

Dockland Striking building along the Elbe waterfront and resembling a ship moored at the docks. (pictured; p128)

Tanzende Türme The 'Dancing Towers' at the eastern end of Reeperbahn. (p108)

HafenCity Futuristic architecture with a special focus on sustainable construction (p93).

Unesco Recognition

Unesco recognised Speicherstadt's ground-breaking architectural imprint in 2015, including within the citation the buildings of Hamburg's Kontorhaus District, one of Europe's first purpose-built office building developments. It's dominated by the Chilehaus (p45), which is alongside other so-called Backsteingotik buildings

For Kids

Hamburg is a fairly child-friendly city, although options are limited when the weather closes in. Depending on the age of your child, harbour tours, festivals, football games and some of the museums are highlights, while the chance to get up high and look down on the city is something most kids enjoy.

Museums

Many of Hamburg's museums are child-friendly, though not all. Some even seem designed to appeal to kids above all others.

Tours & Entertainment

Not all tours work for kids but a handful do. Otherwise, there's football, a scary amusement park and row boats to enjoy.

Viewpoints & Architecture

Getting above it all for seemingly endless views appeals to many kids, as does architecture that seems to have sprung from a child's imagination.

Best Museums

Chocoversum Hamburg's very own chocolate museum is all about indulgence; design your own chocolate bar. (p48)

Miniatur Wunderland This near-perfect display of Hamburg in miniature is a favourite of kids and the young at heart. (p90)

Internationales Maritimes Museum Hamburg's maritime museum has many calling cards but the 26,000 model ships are the stuff of some kids' dreams. (pictured; p88)

Museum für Hamburgische Geschichte Model ships and working model trains take kids on a journey through Hamburg's history. (p108)

Panoptikum If all else fails, there's always the wax museum – more than 120 figures include some they'll recognise. (p109)

Tierpark Hagenbeck Hamburg's zoo is a little out of the centre but the kids will thank you for making the trek. (p99)

Best Tours & Entertainment

Barclaycard Arena Football-mad kids won't want to miss a Bundesliga match if there's one on. (p128)

BILDAGENTUR-ONLINE/JOKO/ALAMY ©

Hamburg Dungeon If your child's over 10 years old and not easily scared, try this amusement park. (p95)

Beatles Tour St Pauli's not for the innocent, but a Beatles Tour can be loads of fun for older kids. (p110)

Harbour Tour (p25) Take a boat tour and enjoy a whole new perspective on the city, hopping on and off. (p25)

Segelschule Pieper Rent a row boat or paddleboat if the weather's fine. (p77)

HafenCity Riverbus Hamburg's only amphibious bus tour... (p96)

Best Viewpoints & Architecture

Mahnmal St-Nikolai A prime contender for Ham-

burg's best views, reached via a glass elevator. (p38)

St Michaelis Kirche Getting the kids to church is easy when there are steeple views like this on offer. (p58)

Altonaer Balkon Some kids could stay here all day watching the ships come and go. (p128)

Elbphilharmonie Eye-catching architectural showpiece that leaves kids looking in wonder. (p86)

Dockland Is it a boat or a building? Let your kids decide then climb to the roof. (p128)

Tanzende Türme Reeperbahn isn't really for kids, but these 'Dancing Towers' watch over the entrance. (p108)

Top Tips

Transport Children under six travel free. The '9-Uhr-Tageskarte' (€6.40) is valid for nine hours for one adult and up to three children. A single-trip ticket for kids aged six to 14 is €1.20.

Restaurants Most places are child-friendly, some have kids menus, and most have a limited number of high chairs.

Entertainment

Hamburg's throbbing entertainment scene is one of the most diverse you'll find anywhere. From some of the finest classical music stages in the country and top-notch German-language theatre, to the down-and-dirty stages of St Pauli, there's always something going on, whatever your taste. For more information, visit www.piste.de/hamburg or www.szene-hamburg.com.

Live Music

Hamburg has a happening live music scene, and it has long been a fixture on the European circuit for major international acts. It also has a reputation for fostering up-and-coming performers.

Theatre

Big, glossy Broadway and West End productions are immensely popular in Hamburg, the nation's 'musical capital'. The tourist offices have plenty of information on the big shows, while ticket offices have highly visible shopfronts around the city. There are also a number of venues for traditional theatre.

Best by Neighbourhood

Altstadt Little after-dark action but at least one live venue. (p54)

Neustadt A handful of live venues with the state opera and classical music. (p68)

St Georg A few gay venues are supplemented by one of the city's best theatres. (p82)

Speicherstadt & Hafen-City Home to the peerless Elbphilharmonie, a fab classical concert venue. (p99)

St Pauli & Reeperbahn The hub of Hamburg's live music scene. (p118)

Altona & Elbmeile Home to an excellent live venue and an arthouse cinema. (p134)

Best Live Performances

Elbphilharmonie World-class venue with jaw-dropping architecture. (p86)

Gruenspan Terrific live venue in St Pauli with regular class acts. (p118)

Mojo Club Hamburg's best jazz stage in a fun and funky setting. (p118)

Knust Legendary St Pauli stage open to all genres. (p120)

Fabrik You could find anything happening at this dynamic place. (p134)

Barclaycard Arena Watch Bundesliga games at Hamburger SV's home. (p128)

PANTHER MEDIA GMBH/ALAMY ©

Best Classical Music

Elbphilharmonie A world-class stage. (p86)

Staatsoper Home of Hamburg's prestigious state opera. (p68)

Laeiszhalle There's so much happening in Hamburg, classical performances overflow here. (p69)

Best Live Music

Gruenspan St Pauli's best live music venue among many. (p118)

Mojo Club Basement jazz for first-class acts. (p118)

Knust Terrific place for all manner of live acts. (pictured; p120)

Fabrik Another eclectic place that showcases

Hamburg's diversity of live performances. (p134)

Cascadas Soul, jazz, Latin, funk, Caribbean and blues in Altstadt. (p54)

Hasenschaukel In the finest St Pauli tradition of indie and up-and-coming acts. (p118)

Best Music Festivals

MS Dockville August festival south of the Elbe with a stellar line-up year in, year out. (p55)

Reeperbahn Festival All kinds of music appears here, which is *very* Reeperbahn. (p120)

Schlagermove Celebration of 1970s German rock with dress-ups. (p120)

Altonale Neighbourhood street festival with live music front and centre. (p132)

Best Theatres

The English Theatre of Hamburg Quality English-language drama north of the centre. (p80)

Deutsches Schauspielhaus Theatre Hamburg's best stage for German-language performances. (p82)

St Pauli Theater A mix of mainstream and offbeat plays in the heart of St Pauli. (p118)

Schmidt Tivoli All manner of plays and performances with a St Pauli love of the mischievous. (p119)

Zeise Kino Arthouse cinema in Altona. (p134)

Activities

Taking a boat ride or harbour tour is the most popular activity. There are plenty of opportunities for walking, although few green spaces in which to do it. On the other hand, the city is bicycle-friendly with plenty of bike lanes and widely accessible rental options.

BILDAGENTUR-ONLINE/JOKO/ALAMY ©

Best Activities

ATG Alster-Touristik A waterborne version of the hop-on, hop-off sightseeing phenomenon. (p65)

Zweiradperle Centrally located bicycle rental with information on routes. (p140)

Segelschule Pieper Get out onto the water under your own steam, then sit back and admire the view. (p77)

Maritime Circle Line Another option for exploring the city from the water. (p110)

Best Places for a Walk

Baakenpark An oasis of green at the southeastern end of HafenCity with terrific water views. (p97)

Süllberg Hill The best views of the Elbe (nearly 3km wide

here) and its container ships are from the 75m-high Süllberg hill. Take the S-Bahn to Blankenese, then bus 48 to Waseberg. (p135)

Altonaer Balkon Pretty park overlooking the Elbe west of the city centre. (pictured; p128)

Park Fiction Elbe-side walks with plenty of shade. (p109)

Tours

Taking a guided tour is an excellent way to both get an overview of Hamburg and zero in on those aspects of the city that appeal. Walking tours are a particular favourite (most advertise as being free, but a €5 to €10 per person tip is appreciated). There are also harbour and bus tours.

FOTOS593/SHUTTERSTOCK ©

Boat Tours

For port tours, it's easiest to just go to Landungsbrücken and pick a boat that's leaving when you want.

Walking Tours

Dozens of walking tours operate throughout the city, many with specific themes, such as redlight tours, 'historic hooker' tours, culinary tours and more. Tourist offices have full details.

Bus Tours

You can hop on and hop off numerous bus tour companies using the same ticket. Route A is by far the best and most popular.

Best Boat Tours

Abicht Popular harbour tours, including Saturday-evening tours past the illuminated warehouses. (p111)

Barkassen-Centrale Ehlers One- or two-hour harbour tours, as well as canal and specialised trips in historic boats. (p64)

Hadag Harbour tours plus more adventuresome trips to the Lower Elbe. (p111)

Maritime Circle Line Harbour shuttle service connecting Hamburg's maritime attractions. (p110)

HafenCity Riverbus A 70-minute tour of the city in an amphibious bus. (p96)

Best Walking Tours

Abenteuer Hamburg Various tours are on offer here, including St Pauli adults-only 'Sex & Crime' tour. (p111)

Beatles Tour A fun and intersting tour about the Beatles in Hamburg. It includes museum entry and a small concert. (p110)

Hamburg Touren Tours to the Elbphilharmonie, 'St Pauli by Night' and 'Sex, Drugs & Currywurst' tours. (p111)

Hamburg Walks Well-run tours covering most of the city centre in three hours. (p48)

Robin & the Tour Guides (www.robinandthetour guides.de) Free two-hour 'Historic City Centre' tours, amongst other tours.

LGBT+

Hamburg is popular with schwule (gay) and lesbische (lesbian) travellers, with the rainbow flag flying especially proudly in St Georg, particularly surrounding Lange Reihe. Public displays of affection may attract unwanted attention in some areas though, including the Steindamm and Hansaplatz areas of St Georg.

DANIEL REINHARDT/DPA/ALAMY ©

Entertainment

Hamburg has a thriving gay and lesbian scene. Much of the action is centred on the St Georg area but mixed venues are found across the city and, in essence, the 'gay and lesbian friendly' label could be applied to most nightspots in the city.

For more information, men can find information at the gay centre **Hein & Fiete** (www.heinfiete.de; Pulverteich 21; ⏰4-9pm Mon-Fri, to 7pm Sat;

Ⓤ Hauptbahnhof-Süd) in St Georg, while women can contact the lesbian centre **Intervention** (www.intervention-hamburg.de; Glashüttenstrasse 2; ⏰hours vary; Ⓤ Feldstrasse) in St Pauli.

Useful guides to Hamburg's gay and lesbian entertainment scene include:

Blu (www.blu.fm) Free print and online magazine with searchable, up-to-the-minute location and event listings.

Hinnerk (www.hinnerk.de) Good for gay venues around the city.

L-Mag (www.l-mag.de) Bimonthly magazine for lesbians. Available at newsagents.

Patroc Gay Travel Guide (www.patroc.com/hamburg) Travel information for 25 European destinations, including Hamburg.

Spartacus International Gay Guide (https://spartacus.gayguide.travel) Annual English-language travel guide for men. Available online, in bookstores and app.

Travel Gay Europe (www.travelgayeurope.com/destination/gay-germany/gay-hamburg) Decent gay guide for the city.

For Free

You don't get much for free in Hamburg these days, but there are still plenty of ways to keep costs down, from discount cards that reduce entry and transport fees considerably to cheaper days at some museums. Many city tours advertise as being for free, and they are if you decide not to tip.

HELGALVIV/SHUTTERSTOCK ©

Best Free Experiences

Elbphilharmonie Fabulous architecture, glorious views and a generally unforgettable experience. (p86)

Fischmarkt Lively Sunday-morning market down by the waterfront. (p102)

Rathaus You'll need to take the tour for the full glory, but the facade and the entrance hall can be enjoyed for nothing. (pictured; p42)

HafenCity InfoCenter Terrific introduction to Hamburg's most dynamic corner. (p93)

St Pauli Nachtmarkt You'll end up spending money at the stalls but it costs nothing to enjoy the atmosphere. (p108)

HafenCity Nachhaltigkeitspavillon Intriguing look at sustainable construction in the HafenCity story. (p93)

Best Free Hamburg Icons

Davidwache St Pauli police station and TV star in its own right. (p105)

Beatles-Platz Honour the Beatles along Reeperbahn, itself a free icon. (p108)

Altonaer Balkon Take in the Elbe from one of its finest vantage points. (p128)

Rote Flora Counterculture, graffiti and attitude. (p128)

Deichstrasse Old Hamburg's prettiest corner with gables and cobblestones. (p45)

Four Perfect Days

Day 1

SCIROCCO340/SHUTTERSTOCK ©

Begin in the centre of town with breakfast at **Café Paris** (p45), admiring the **Rathaus** (p42) and **Chilehaus** (pictured; p45), before visiting **Mahnmal St-Nikolai** (p38) for its museum and fabulous views.

Wander along picturesque **Deichstrasse** (p45), then lunch at **Deichgraf** (p51), **Alt Hamburger Aalspeicher** (p45) or **Kartoffelkeller** (p50). Walk down to Landungsbrücke for a harbour tour aboard the hop-on, hop-off ferry.

Return to Altstadt for dinner at **Daniel Wischer** (p51) or currywurst at **Mö-Grill** (p49). Follow up with a beer at **Gröninger Privatbrauerei** (p45), then a classy cocktail at **Le Lion** (p53), all-night dancing at **Nachtasyl** (p54) and/or live music at **Cascadas** (p54).

Day 2

LOOK DIE BILDAGENTUR DER FOTOGRAFEN GMBH/ALAMY ©

Start in St Georg with breakfast at **Café Gnosa** (p75) along Lange Reihe with its boutiques and craft workshops. The **Museum für Kunst und Gewerbe** (p77) is worth an hour or two. Stop for lunch at **Café Koppel** (p75).

Follow a coffee or cocktail at **a.mora** (p80) with **Hamburger Kunsthalle** (pictured; p40). Then take to the water, renting a row boat to tour through **Segelschule Pieper** (p77).

Head over to St Pauli for dinner at **Clouds** (p113). Wander along Reeperbahn to get your bearings, then dive into the nightlife with a beer at **Zur Ritze** (p114) or **Zum Silbersack** (p105), perhaps a high-class jazz show at **Mojo Club** (p118), and all-night dancing at **Molotow** (p115).

Day 3

TILMAN EHRICKE/SHUTTERSTOCK ©

Out in Neustadt's west, wander the boutiques and restaurants of Wexstrasse, pause at **Public Coffee Roasters** (p61), then visit the **Johannes Brahms Museum** (p61), **Komponisten-Quartier** (p61) and **Kramer-amtswohnungen** (p63), before climbing **St Michaelis Kirche** (pictured; p58). Lunch at **Old Commercial Room** (p65).

In Speicherstadt, **Miniatur Wunderland** (p90), **Speicherstadt Museum** (p93) and **Internationales Maritimes Museum** (p88) are all excellent. As evening approaches, head for **Elbphilharmonie** (p86) and perhaps even book a show. Dine at **Fischerhaus** (p113).

Back over in St Pauli, try some classic neighbourhood bars, such as **Golden Pudel Club** (p114), **Indra Club** (p115) or **Lunacy** (p105).

Day 4

PANTHER MEDIA GMBH/ALAMY ©

There are few places where we'd rather spend a Hamburg morning than in Altona. Begin with breakfast at **Mikkels** (p125), take in the views from **Altonaer Balkon** (p128), then lunch at **Atlantik Fisch** (p132) or **Von Der Motte** (p131).

Catch the S-Bahn and spend the afternoon shopping in Neustadt, stopping often in the elegant cafes beneath the arches and alongside the canals.

By 6pm you'll need to be at the Feldstrasse U-Bahn station for the fun-filled **Beatles Tour** (p110); either have an early dinner beforehand, or eat afterwards at **Nil** (p114) or **Brachmanns Galeron** (p113). Follow up with live music at **Knust** (pictured; p120), or bunker down for all-night dancing in the surreal **Uebel und Gefährlich** (p117).

Need to Know

For detailed information, see Survival Guide p137

Population
1.8 million

Currency
Euro (€)

Language
German

Money
ATMs widely available. Credit/debit cards widely accepted, but bring emergency cash.

Time
Central European Time (GMT/UTC plus one hour)

Visas
Generally not required for stays of up to 90 days per 180 days (visas are not required at all for members of EU or Schengen countries). Some nationalities need a Schengen visa.

Mobile Phones
Mobile phones operate on GSM900/1800. If you have a European or Australian phone, save money by slipping in a German SIM card.

Daily Budget

Budget: Less than €100
Hostel or private room: €20–40
Cheap meal: up to €8
Museums: free–€10

Midrange: €100–200
Private apartment or double room: €60–100
Three-course dinner at a nice restaurant: €30–40
Couple of beers in a pub or beer garden: €8

Top End: More than €200
Fancy loft apartment or double in a top-end hotel: from €150
Sit-down lunch and dinner at a top-rated restaurant: €100
Concert or opera tickets: €50-150

Advance Planning

Three months before Look for hotel deals and book your room. Check out Elbphilharmonie's (p86) concert program.

One month before Reserve your table at Die Bank (p67) or Clouds (p113), two of Hamburg's most prestigious tables. This is especially true if your visit coincides with a weekend.

One week before Reserve your spot on one of the tours such as the Beatles Tour (p110) or Hamburg Touren (p111).

Arriving in Hamburg

✈ From Hamburg Airport

The S1 S-Bahn connects the airport directly with the city centre. The journey takes 25 minutes and costs €3.30. Taxis cost €20 to €30 and take around 30 minutes, longer during peak hour.

🚉 From Hamburg Hauptbahnhof

The main train station is in the heart of the city and within walking distance of many hotels. Otherwise take the subway, for which a single ticket costs €3.30.

Getting Around

Hamburg is a big place, so you'll likely use more than your feet to explore the city. Thankfully there's an excellent public transport system in place to get you where you want to go.

🚉 Train

Colour-coded rail and subway lines that criss-cross the city are likely your most convenient way of getting around, including travel to/from the airport.

🚲 Bicycle

Hamburg is a very bike-friendly city with plenty of places for renting your own wheels.

🚌 Bus

An extensive system that has the city centre and beyond covered, but you'll need to plan carefully to understand the routes.

🚕 Taxi

Reasonably expensive but good if you're in a hurry or have lots of luggage.

RSPHOTOGRAPHY/SHUTTERSTOCK ©

Hamburg Neighbourhoods

Altona & Elbmeile (p123)

Much-loved residential zone rising from the Elbe's shoreline, filled with neighbourhood bars and restaurants.

Fischmarkt

St Pauli & Reeperbahn (p101)

Louche and life-filled, St Pauli and Reeperbahn are where Hamburg gets up close and personal.

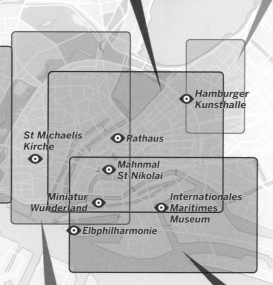

Altstadt (p37)

Old Hamburg is the city in microcosm, with medieval architecture and storied bars and restaurants.

St Georg (p73)

Alternative St Georg is the city's most artistic corner, with fabulous places to eat, drink and shop.

St Michaelis Kirche ◉

◉ **Rathaus**

◉ **Hamburger Kunsthalle**

◉ **Mahnmal St-Nikolai**

Miniatur Wunderland ◉

Internationales Maritimes Museum ◉

◉ **Elbphilharmonie**

Neustadt (p57)

Hamburg at its most elegant, Neustadt is rich in museums, glamorous boutiques and waterfront charm.

Speicherstadt & HafenCity (p85)

Hamburg's docks district is a happening place with countless museums and a stunning architectural showpiece.

Explore
Hamburg

Walkway near the Elbphilharmonie (p86) CLAUDIO DIVIZIA/SHUTTERSTOCK ©

Explore ✦

Altstadt

Altstadt, the heart of Old Hamburg, is awash with beautiful facades, soaring churches and a magnificent town hall. But it's also home to an underrated range of terrific eateries to suit a variety of budgets, as well as good shopping and some excellent bars. There aren't many places to stay here, but you'll find yourself passing through again and again.

Begin your day with breakfast at Café Paris (p45) and a walk along the waterfront as the city comes to life. You'll need the best part of the rest of the day to take in all of the sights, ticking off the Rathaus (p42), Hamburger Kunsthalle (p40), Chilehaus (p45), Chocoversum (p48) and Mahnmal St-Nikolai (p38). Leave the latter until last, and combine it with a stroll, a coffee and a meal along Deichstrasse (p45). And try to end up at the inner harbour late afternoon or early evening when the waterfront again throngs with locals on their way home and tourists catching boats.

Getting There & Around

Ⓤ & Ⓢ The Mönckebergstrasse (line U3) and Rathaus (U3) are both in the heart of Altstadt. Jungfernstieg (lines S1, S2, S3, U1, U2 and U3), Hauptbahnhof-Süd (U1 and U3) and Hauptbahnhof-Nord (U2 and U4) are all major transit hubs and lie around the neighbourhood's perimeter. Other useful stations include Messberg (U1), Steinstrasse (U1) and Rödingsmarkt (U3).

Altstadt Map on p46

View of the Rathaus from Alsterarkaden (p64) IAN DAGNALL/ALAMY ©

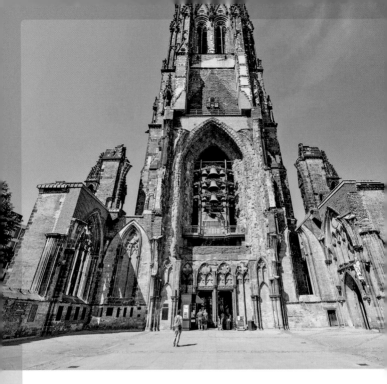

Top Sights 📷
Mahnmal St-Nikolai

At once haunting and soaring, this half ruin is one of Hamburg's most distinctive sights. There's an outstanding museum devoted to the devastation of war, and the views from the tower's summit rank among Hamburg's finest. It's this combination of a sobering story and the uplifting experience of rising above it all that gives Mahnmal St-Nikolai (Memorial of St Nicholas) its cachet.

◎ **MAP P46, C5**

☏ 040-371 125

www.mahnmal-st-nikolai.de

Willy-Brandt-Strasse 60

adult/child €5/3

🕑 10am-6pm May-Sep, to 5pm Oct-Apr

Ⓤ Rödingsmarkt

Architecture & History

This church was first built in 1195, taking decades to complete. In 1943, it took only minutes to reduce it to rubble. Difficult as it is to imagine now, the church of St-Nikolai was the world's tallest building from 1874 to 1876. Even today, it remains Hamburg's second-tallest structure (after the TV tower that you'll often see on the horizon away to the north). In 1943 an Allied bombardment destroyed all but the tower. What remains is at once magnificent and profoundly disturbing.

Anti-War Museum

Down in the basement, just to one side of the concourse (or what would have been the church's main sanctuary), the Mahnmal St-Nikolai museum's exhibition focuses on three events in World War II: the German bombing of Coventry in 1940; the German destruction of Warsaw, and Operation Gomorrah, the combined British and American bombing of Hamburg over three days and nights in 1943, which killed 35,000 citizens and incinerated much of the centre.

Great Glass Elevator

The highlight for many visitors is the glass lift up to a 76.3m-high viewing platform inside the surviving spire, for views of Hamburg's centre, put into context of the wartime destruction. The views are all-encompassing and utterly breathtaking. From up here, Hamburg's watery personality is fully apparent, and the view of the harbour – all ships and silhouettes – is offset by the epoch-defining Elbphilharmonie, which, it must be said, is very difficult to take your eyes off.

★ Top Tips

o Note that St-Nikolai remains open despite any scaffolding for reconstruction – you wouldn't be the first visitor to turn away thinking it was closed!

o Get here as close to opening time as you can – the queues can be long throughout the day, and only so many people can fit in the elevator at any one time.

o If you're keen to see Hamburg at its best, visit as close to sunset as the opening hours allow to see the city bathed in golden light.

✗ Take a Break

Wander down to charming Deichstrasse for some of Hamburg's best coffee at Nord Coast Coffee Roasters (p54).

For something more substantial, discover the local passion for potatoes at Kartoffelkeller (p50).

Top Sights 📷
Hamburger Kunsthalle

Hamburg's best and most prestigious art gallery is also one of Germany's best. While the focus, particularly in the pieces dating back to medieval times, is overwhelmingly on German art, the gallery also has a fine collection of masters from further afield. The contemporary collection is as outstanding as the earlier works and the stunning architecture perfectly complements the collection throughout.

◉ MAP P46, F1

☎ 040-428 131 200

www.hamburger-kunsthalle.de

Glockengiesserwall

adult/child €14/free, 🕑 10am-6pm Tue, Wed & Fri-Sun, to 9pm Thu

Ⓤ Hauptbahnhof-Nord

Old Masters

Right from the chronological starting point of the museum's collection, things get serious. Amid the numerous examples of religious triptych and other sacred pieces, some names stand out (and confirm that the collection is not restricted to German artists): Lucas Cranach the Younger, Francisco José de Goya y Lucientes, Peter Paul Rubens and Giovanni Battista Tiepolo, to name just a few.

19th-Century Art

The 19th century was a golden age for European art and many of its most significant standard bearers are represented here. Again, they're a pretty international lot: Edgar Degas, Caspar David Friedrich, Max Liebermann, Edouard Manet, Claude Monet and Auguste Rodin. Paintings that stand out include Paul Gauguin's *Breton Boys Bathing* and Friedrich's *Wanderer above the Sea of Fog*.

Classical Modernism

This gallery is devoted to the late 19th and early 20th century until the 1970s, a period distinguished by a clear break from the artistic traditions of the past. It's a pretty elite group that includes such luminaries as Francis Bacon, Max Ernst, Paul Klee, Edvard Munch and, everybody's favourite, Pablo Picasso. Munch's *Madonna* and Klee's *Revolution of the Viaduct* capture the astonishing range of styles within this gallery.

Gegenwart & Contemporary Art

The museum's collection of contemporary art has found the perfect home, the cube-like and utterly contemporary Galerie der Gegenwart, built in 1997. It's the ideal venue for works by, among others, Rebecca Horn, Georg Baselitz and Gerhard Richter, as well as international stars including David Hockney, Jeff Koons, Tracey Emin and Andy Warhol.

★ **Top Tips**

o Don't plan to visit the gallery on a Monday (it's closed). If that's your only day in Hamburg, aaargh!

o Keep an eye out for temporary exhibitions, such is the prestige of the Hamburger Kunsthalle that it attracts world-class touring exhibitions.

o The museum stays open later on Thursday nights and is cheaper, but it can be crowded as a result.

o The usual adult admission fee of €14 is reduced to €10 with the Hamburg Card (p144), and is free with the Hamburg City Pass (p144).

✕ **Take a Break**

Ahoi by Steffen Henssler (p50), 10 minutes away, has the advantage of being both fast food and good for sit-down meals.

Lovers of currywurst will enjoy that Mö-Grill (p49) is just 10 minutes from the museum on foot.

Top Sights 📷
Rathaus

*With its gilded facade and spectacular coffered
ceiling, Hamburg's baroque Rathaus (town hall)
is one of Europe's most opulent. It's also unusual
in that both the facade and the interior are equally
beautiful. Visits occur as part of a 40-minute tour,
which takes in only a fraction of this beehive of
647 rooms.*

◎ MAP P46, D3

📞 040-428 3124

Rathausmarkt 1

tours adult/under 14yr
€5/free; half-hourly 11am-
4pm Mon-Fri, 10am-5pm
Sat, to 4pm Sun

Ⓤ Rathausmarkt,
Jungfernstieg,
Ⓢ Jungfernstieg

The Facade

Despite the apparent medieval extravagance of the facade, the Rathaus was actually only built in the late 19th century. But this feeling is no accident – it was built in a neo-Renaissance style, well suited to the neighbouring buildings in Neustadt. Crowned by a 112m-high tower, the facade is especially beautiful for its balcony upon which is depicted Hammonia, Hamburg's patron goddess, and the city's coat of arms.

The Entrance

The main entrance, which includes an elaborate wrought-iron gate, has a roof supported by more than a dozen sandstone columns. Note the portraits of Hamburg's great and good that hang on the walls, and the Sicilian marble staircase.

Emperor's Hall

One of the Rathaus's most hallowed spaces – the Emperor's or Imperial Hall (*Kaisersaal*), is so named because of a visit to the Rathaus by Kaiser Wilhelm II in 1895. The ceiling fresco is stunning while the wall has unusual leather coverings. The adjacent Tower Hall is still used for ceremonial occasions.

Other Halls

To leave your mark on posterity, sign the Golden Book in the Mayor's Hall. The Phoenix Hall takes its name from the phoenix above the hearth, which symbolises Hamburg's rebirth after the great fire of 1842. In the Senate chamber, there are no windows but light floods in from the glass roof; in ancient German custom, councils were only to meet in the open air.

Grand Ballroom

The pinnacle of the Rathaus' splendour is the grand ballroom, and most tours leave the best until last. Nearly 50m long, the ballroom is hung with vast paintings that tell 1200 years of Hamburg history.

★ **Top Tips**

o Most tours are conducted in German but English is used if there's enough demand – try and get a group of you together if possible.

o Early morning is the best time to photograph the facade, bathed in golden light; by afternoon, the facade is in shadow.

o All tours are busy, but the first one of the morning may be a little less crowded.

✕ **Take a Break**

One of the city's oldest purveyors of fine fish, Daniel Wischer (p51), is within sight of the Rathaus and does sit-down meals and fish and chips to take away.

Elegant Café Paris (p45) is good at any time of the day, but breakfast is its strong suit.

Walking Tour 🥾

Heart of Old Hamburg

If there is one unifying theme in Altstadt, a place where all of Hamburg comes together without leaving behind any discernible neighbourhood personality, it is holding fast to surviving relics of the past and celebrating them. Whether in the realm of food or architecture, the effect is one of preserving traditions for the city as a whole.

Walk Facts

Start Chilehaus;
⑤ Messberg

End Gröninger Privatbrauerei;
Ⓤ Messberg

Length 1.5km

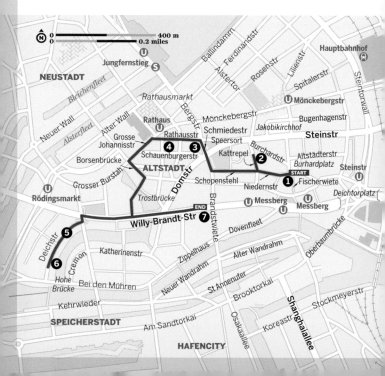

❶ Chilehaus

One of Hamburg's most beautiful buildings is crowning gem of the new Unesco-anointed Kontorhaus District. The 1924 **Chilehaus** (📞040-349 194 247; www.chilehaus.de; Fischertwiete 2) is shaped like an ocean liner, with curved walls meeting in the shape of a ship's bow and staggered balconies like decks. It's a prime example of German expressionist architecture, with other *Backsteingotik* (brick gothic) buildings nearby.

❷ Laufauf

A bastion for northern German and Hamburg cooking, **Laufauf** (📞040-326 626; www.laufauf.de; Kattrepel 2; mains €10.50-16; ⏰noon-10pm Mon-Sat) is something of a Hamburg institution. The *pannfisch* (locally fried fish), *bratheringe* (fried herring) and *labskaus* (a meat, fish and potato stew with beetroot) are particularly good. It's a pretty casual place, with a mostly local crowd.

❸ Hamburger SV City Store

Fans of SV Hamburg, the city's most successful football team and those looking for a souvenir for a football-mad friend back home can head to this Altstadt **store** (📞040-4155 1887; www.hsv.de/de/fanshop/fanshops; Schmiedestrasse 2; ⏰10am-7pm Mon-Fri, to 4pm Sat). It sells football shirts, scarves and other memorabilia.

❹ Café Paris

Within a spectacularly tiled 1882 butchers' hall and adjoining art-deco salon, this elegant yet relaxed **brasserie** (📞040-3252 7778; www.cafeparis.net; Rathausstrasse 4; mains €15-26; ⏰9am-11.30pm) serves classical French fare like *croque-monsieur* (toasted ham-and-cheese sandwich), and steak tartare (minced meat, but pan-fried, not raw). Its breakfast for two is a splendid feast.

❺ Deichstrasse

Hamburg's Great Fire of 1842 broke out in **Deichstrasse**, which features a few restored 18th-century homes, most now housing restaurants. You can get a feel for the old canal and merchants' quarter here.

❻ Alt Hamburger Aalspeicher

The knick-knack-filled dining room and warm service at this **restaurant** (📞040-362 990; www.aalspeicher.de; Deichstrasse 43; mains €13-27; ⏰noon-11pm Wed-Sun), in a 400-year-old canalside building, make you feel like you're dining in your *Oma's* (grandma's) house . Smoked eel from its own smoke-house is a speciality.

❼ Gröninger Privatbrauerei

Drink in one of Hamburg's oldest **breweries** (📞040-570 105 100; www.groeninger-hamburg.de; Willy Brandt Strasse 47; ⏰11am-midnight Mon-Fri, 5pm-midnight Sat, 3-10pm Sun). If you get the munchies, their pork knuckles served with crackling is *the* order.

For reviews see

◉ Top Sights	p38
◉ Sights	p48
⊗ Eating	p49
⊙ Drinking	p53
✪ Entertainment	p54
⊡ Shopping	p54

200 m
0.1 miles

Grosse Theaterstr

Colonnaden

Neuer Jungfernstieg

Gänsemarkt

Gänsemarkt

ABC Str

Hohe Bleichen

Jungfernstieg

Hanseviertel

Jungfernstieg

Jungfernstieg

Kaiser-Wilhelm-Str

Fuhlentwiete

Grosse Bleichen

Poststr

NEUSTADT

Bleichenbrücke

Adolfsbrücke

Bleichenfleet

13

23

5

Rathausmarkt

Alsterfleet

Hamburg Walks

Wexstr

Alter Wall

Rathaus

Alter Steinweg

Neuer Wall

Rathaus

Grosse Johannisstr

16

Stadthausbrücke

Graskeller

Rathausstr

11

Schauenburgerstr

ALTSTADT

Ludwig-Erhard-Str

Rödingsmarkt

Grosser Burstah

Börsenbrücke

Trostbrücke

Trostbrücke

Stubbenhuk-Herrengraben

Alsterfleet

21

Rödingsmarkt

Mahnmal St-Nikolai

Schaartor

Deichstr

18

10

12

Cremon

15

Katherinenstr

Baumwall

Baumwall

Kajen

Hohe Brücke

Bei den Mühren

Neuer Wandrahm

Kehrwieder

SPEICHERSTADT

E Lombardsbrücke
F
G
H

ST GEORG

Lange Reihe

1

Holzdamm

Binnenalster

Glockengiesserwall

Hamburger Kunsthalle

20

Kirchenallee

Ernst-Merck-Str

Ballindamm

Hachmannplatz

Hauptbahnhof-Nord U Bremer Reihe

2

Ferdinandstr

Raboisen

Lilienstr

Hauptbahnhof S Hauptbahnhof

Hauptbahnhof-Süd U

22

Alstertor

Hermannstr

Rosenstr

Steintorplatz

8 Spitalerstr

19

6 U Mönckebergstr

Steintorwall

3

3 *Galerie Commeter*

Mönckebergstr

Jakobikirchhof

Kurt-Schumacher-Allee

U Steinstr

Steinstr

Speersort

17

Steinstr

Zweiradperle 4

Johanniswall

Domstr

Burchardstr

Kattrepel

Altstädterstr

Burhardplatz

4

Schopenstehl

7

Niedernstr

Steinstr U

Kleine Reichenstr

9

Kingberg

1 Pumpen

U

Messberg

U

Chocoversum

Deichtorplatz

Willy-Brandt-Str

U

Brandstwiete

Messberg

Oberbaumbrücke

Poggenmühlenbrücke

Deichtorstr

Dovenfleet

14

2

5

Alter Wandrahm

Deichtorhallen

Zippelhaus

Oberhafenbrüke

St. Annenufer

Brooktorkai

Stockmeyerstr

6

HAFENCITY

Koreastr

E
F
G
H

Sights

The centre of old Hamburg is also the hub of the modern city. Largely reconstructed after WWII, the city's ages-old wealth is apparent as you stroll among its most important civic and commercial institutions. In Hanseatic times, this was where you found the rich merchants and their businesses along the canals.

The attractions are spread out across the neighbourhood, and although it's not the largest geographically, it's a good 15- to 20-minute walk from one end (the Hamburger Kunsthalle) to the other (Deichstrasse). The latter is easily combined with Mahnmal St-Nikolai, with the rest close to the waterfront.

Chocoversum   MUSEUM

1 ⊙ MAP P46, F4

Who needs an excuse to fall in love with chocolate? This fun museum involves a 90-minute guided tour through the world of chocolate and even lets you design your own chocolate bar. Kids will love it – we did, too. (☏040-4191 2300; www.chocoversum.de; Messberg 1; adult/child €12/10; ⏰10am-6pm; Ⓤ Messberg)

Deichtorhallen   GALLERY

2 ⊙ MAP P46, G5

Two grandly restored brick market halls, built in 1911 and 1913 respectively, are home to high-profile special exhibitions of modern art and photography. (Hall of Contemporary Art, House of Photography; ☏040-321 030; www.deichtorhallen. de; Deichtorstrasse 1-2; adult/child €10/free; ⏰11am-6pm Tue-Sun; Ⓢ Steinstrasse)

Galerie Commeter   GALLERY

3 ⊙ MAP P46, E3

Founded in 1821, privately run Galerie Commeter is Hamburg's oldest gallery, with a reliable offering of contemporary painting, graphics, sculpture and photography. (☏040-326 321; www.commeter. de; Bergstrasse 11; admission free; ⏰11am-6pm Tue-Fri, to 4pm Sat; Ⓤ Rathaus)

Zweiradperle   CYCLING

4 ⊙ MAP P46, G4

Offers a range of rental bikes (including helmets and locks), as well as tours. The three-hour tour is a great introduction to the city. Has a cool cafe and plenty of cycling info. In 2017 they opened a new outpost in St Pauli. (☏040-3037 3474; www.zweiradperle.hamburg; Altstädter Strasse 3-7; rental per day from €14, tour incl rental from €25; ⏰10am-6pm daily Apr–mid-Oct, 11am-6pm Tue-Fri, to 3pm Sat mid-Oct–Mar, tour 10.30am daily; Ⓤ Steinstrasse)

Hamburg Walks   TOURS

5 ⊙ MAP P46, D3

These well-run tours cover most of the city centre in three hours, with plenty of historical detail and local stories. (www.hamburgwalks.de; Schleusenbrücke 1; adult/concession €14/12; ⏰10.30am Mon, Wed & Fri-Sun; Ⓢ Rathaus, Jungfernstieg)

Eating

Many of the restaurants in the Altstadt cater to bankers and other office workers. There are alternatives, including Deichstrasse, which is lined with atmospheric old buildings – a rarity in this area despite the neighbourhood's name.

Local specialities are something of a recurring theme, making Altstadt a terrific place to try regional cooking. There are also a handful of high-class restaurants where tourists rub shoulders with local gastronomes.

Mö-Grill   GERMAN €

6 ⊗ MAP P46, F3

You can smell the curry and see the crowds from two streets away at this very popular venue for that beloved German fast food, the currywurst. Locals agree that the versions here (and at a second stand across the street) are about the best anywhere. (Mönckebergstrasse 11; mains from €4; ⏱10am-7pm; Ⓤ Mönckebergstrasse)

Goot   GERMAN €

7 ⊗ MAP P46, F4

Top regional ingredients are used in fresh lunches served in a casual setting. There are vegetarian soups and salads plus sandwiches featuring roasted meats. Nab a table outside. (☎040-6730 6171; www.goot-hamburg.de; Depenau 10; mains €7-10; ⏱11.30am-4pm; Ⓤ Messberg)

Chocoversum

BILDAGENTUR-ONLINE/JOKO/ALAMY ©

Ahoi by Steffen Henssler INTERNATIONAL €€

8 ⊗ MAP P46, F3

German-born but always with his eye on the horizon, celebrated local chef Steffen Henssler has made a name for himself as a sushi chef. He also does burgers, salads and even a currywurst. Downstairs at street level you can also get a mean fish and chips (€5.90). (☏040-6466 0560; www. ahoibysteffenhenssler.de; Spitaler-strasse 12; mains from €9.50; ⊗noon-9pm Mon-Sat; Ⓤ Mönckebergstrasse)

Perle Restaurant GERMAN, INTERNATIONAL €€

9 ⊗ MAP P46, F4

Down a quiet Altstadt side street in a pretty terrace house, Perle is especially good at lunchtime with a light menu or daily specials. For dinner, their original Wiener schnitzel is one of the best in town. The base is German, but they're not averse to Argentinian beef or curry sauces. (☏040-5701 6297; www.perle-restaurant.de; Hopfensack 26; mains €9-25; ⊗11.30am-3pm & 6-9pm; Ⓤ Messberg)

Kartoffelkeller GERMAN €€

10 ⊗ MAP P46, C5

One of numerous good choices along pretty Deichstrasse, Kartoffelkeller is true to its name and lives for the potato – *Kartoffelsalate* (potato salad), *Kartoffelpuffer* (potato pancakes), *Kartoffelsuppe* (potato soup), *Pellkartoffel* (jacket potatoes), *Kartoffelknödel* (potato dumplings)… It's all good,

Deichgraf

Hamburg's Concentration Camp

In 1938 the Nazis converted an old brick factory 25km southeast of Hamburg into a concentration camp, **KZ-Gedenkstätte Neuengamme** (Neuengamme Concentration Camp; ☑040-428 131 500; www.kz-gedenkstaette-neuengamme.de; Jean-Dolidier-Weg 75; admission free; ⏱9.30am-4pm Mon-Fri, noon-7pm Sat & Sun Apr-Sep, to 5pm Sat & Sun Oct-Mar). Over the next seven years, countless numbers of people were imprisoned here. At least 42,900 were killed, either murdered directly, or indirectly due to the horrible living conditions. Exhibits recount the Holocaust, both locally and nationally. Only a few historic buildings remain, but the general layout of the huge camp is shown. Take the S-Bahn to Bergedorf, then bus 227 or 327 (about one hour, €8.10).

Much less known than other camps such as Sachsenhausen near Berlin, Neuengamme was only fully opened as a memorial in 2005, after prisons on the site had been closed. Its setting amidst vast expanses of flat farmland adds a mundane horror. You can spend a couple of hours wandering the site, reading the plaques that explain what happened where and going inside surviving buildings for the many exhibits. Combine your time here with a visit to **Bullenhuser Damm Schule** (Bullenhuser Damm School; ☑040-428 1310; www.kz-gedenkstaette-neuengamme.de; Bullenhuser Damm 92-94; admission free; ⏱10am-5pm Sun; Ⓢ Rothenburgsort) in Hamburg for a gruelling window into the horrors of 75 years ago.

although you may wish to not see a potato again for a while. (☑040-365 585; www.kartoffelkeller-hamburg.de; Deichstrasse 21; mains €6-16; ⏱noon-10pm Thu-Tue; Ⓤ Rödingsmarkt)

Daniel Wischer SEAFOOD €€

11 ✗ MAP P46, D4

They've been serving quality fish and chips at Daniel Wischer since the 1920s, and it's a terrific place for a quick meal or something more substantial. Apart from the grilled fish, they do a fantastic fish and chips, or one of Hamburg's best *Fischbrötchen* (fish sandwiches). (☑040-3609 1988; www.danielwischer.de; Grosse Johannisstrasse 3; mains €6.50-17; ⏱11am-9pm Mon-Sat; Ⓤ Steinstrasse)

Deichgraf GERMAN €€€

12 ✗ MAP P46, B5

In a prime setting, with the water on one side and long streetside tables on the other, Deichgraf excels in Hamburg specialities cooked to a high standard. The menu changes seasonally and much of the food is sourced from the region. Their *labskaus* (meat, fish and potato stew) is especially good, and, unusually, they offer a smaller portion for those wanting a taste. (☎040-364 208; www.deichgraf-hamburg.de; Deichstrasse 23; mains €15-26; ☺noon-3pm & 5.30-10pm Mon-Fri, 5.30-10pm Sat; Ⓤ Rödingsmarkt)

Se7en Oceans
SEAFOOD €€€

14 ⊗ MAP P46, D3

At first glance, Se7en Oceans looks like an extension of the food court atop the Europa Passage shopping complex. Look a little closer and you'll find a terrific place with good waterfront views, as well as a sushi bar, cigar lounge, bistro and a gourmet restaurant. The latter's set menus are excellent, while the bistro menu is less imaginative. (☎040-3250 7944; www.se7en-oceans.de; Ballindamm 40, 3rd fl, Europa Passage; restaurant 5-/7-course set menu €99/119, lunch set menus €33-55, bistro mains €9-25; ☺11am-midnight; Ⓤ Jungfernstieg, Ⓢ Jungfernstieg)

Fillet of Soul
FUSION €€€

14 ⊗ MAP P46, G5

Creative fusion cooking is Fillet of Soul's philosophy and meats are the mainstay – the Oldenburger, dry aged beef, is a true classic among carnivores. Influences appear from as far afield as Spain or Japan, and for dessert you simply must try the white chocolate mousse with pineapple carpaccio and mojito sorbet. (☎040-7070 5800; www.fillet-of-soul.de; Deichtorstrasse 2; lunch mains €10-14, dinner mains €17-45; ☺noon-midnight Tue-Sat, to 10pm Sun; Ⓤ Steinstrasse, Messberg)

Trific
GERMAN, INTERNATIONAL €€€

15 ⊗ MAP P46, C5

Consistently lauded as one of Hamburg's more creative kitchens, Trific serves up a small, market- and season-driven menu. When we were there, dishes included beef tartare with truffle mayo, or roasted veal rump. Lovely setting and good service, too. (📞040-4191 9046; www.trific.de; Holzbrücke 7; mains €19-27, 3-/4-course set menu €37/43; 🕐noon-3pm & 6-11pm Mon-Fri, 6-11pm Sat; Ⓤ Rödingsmarkt)

Drinking

While not Hamburg's liveliest neighbourhood after dark, Altstadt does have a small coterie of places to drink, including an elite cocktail bar, one of the city's oldest breweries, a terrific coffee cafe, and a popular nightclub where you can wave your hands in the air.

Le Lion
COCKTAIL BAR

16 🟢 MAP P46, D3

Easily the classiest, most exclusive bar (by virtue of size) you'll find in Hamburg. If there's space and you're nicely dressed, they'll let you into this little lair of serious cocktails – their signature is the gin basil smash. (📞040-334 753 780; www.lelion.net; Rathausstrasse 3; 🕐6pm-3am Mon-Sat, to 1am Sun; Ⓤ Rathaus)

Biergarten Speersort
BEER GARDEN

17 🟢 MAP P46, E4

There's nothing very complicated about this Bavarian-style beer garden or terrace overlooking one of the few green open spaces in the city centre – the outdoor tables are simply a wonderful place to drink beer on a sunny day. (📞040-2788 0060; www.hofbraeu-wirtshaus. de; Speersort 1; 🕐10am-1am Sun-Thu,

Hafengeburtstag celebrations (p55)

ELENA NN/SHUTTERSTOCK ©

to 2am Fri & Sat; U Mönckeberg-strasse, Messberg)

Nord Coast Coffee Roasters COFFEE

18 🚇 MAP P46, C5

One of Hamburg's growing number of cool and socially conscious coffee roasters, Nord Coast has a lovely Deichstrasse location, donates part of its profits to social projects and, yes, makes great coffee as well. (☏ 040-3609 3499; www.nordcoast-coffee.de; Deichstrasse 9; ⊙9am-6pm Mon-Fri, from 10am Sat & Sun)

Nachtasyl CLUB

19 🚇 MAP P46, E3

A mainstay of the Hamburg night, 'Night Asylum' is all about good DJs and a mixed crowd of locals and tourists up for a good time every night of the week. (☏ 040-3281 4207; Alstertor 1-5; cover free-€15; ⊙7pm-late)

Entertainment

Cascadas LIVE MUSIC

20 ⭐ MAP P46, F1

One of the better live music venues outside of St Pauli, Cascadas offers up a nightly program that ranges across soul, jazz, Latin, funk, Caribbean and blues. Things usually get going around 8pm, but check the website for upcoming gigs and times. (www.cascadas.club; Ferdinandstrasse 12; €0-10; ⊙7pm-late)

Shopping

You'll find a little bit of everything when it comes to shopping in Altstadt. The large Europa Passage shopping centre has dozens of local and international brands, but tucked away elsewhere is a handful of boutiques and niche stores. West of the Hauptbahnhof, along Spitalerstrasse and Mönckeberg-strasse (known as the 'Mö'), you'll find the large department stores and mainstream boutiques.

Sleeping Dogs HOMEWARES

21 🔒 MAP P46, B5

This stunning concept store is partly about homeware brands, from local designers to international stars. But just as much thought has gone into the display – it's like an art gallery in here. The look ranges from clean-lined Scandinavian minimalism to vintage classics. (☏ 040-3861 4044; www.sleepingdogs.de; Rödingsmarkt 20; ⊙11am-7pm Mon-Fri, to 4pm Sat; U Rödingsmarkt)

Dr Götze Land & Karte BOOKS

22 🔒 MAP P46, E2

Enormous range of guidebooks and maps. Browse the world. (☏ 040-357 4630; www.landundkarte.de; Alstertor 14-18; ⊙10am-7pm Mon-Fri, to 6pm Sat, 1-6pm Sun; U Mönckebergstrasse, Jungfernstieg; S Jungfernstieg)

Hamburg Festivals

Hafengeburtstag

The city's biggest annual event is this three-day **gala** (Harbour Birthday; www.hamburg.de/hafengeburtstag; ⊘early May). It commemorates Emperor Barbarossa granting Hamburg customs exemption and is energetically celebrated with harbourside concerts, funfairs and gallons of beer. Lots of fun.

Neighbourhood Street Festivals

Spring is the time for local street festivals, when streets are closed off, food trucks converge, live music takes to the stage and there are sometimes flea markets. It begins with the **Osterstrasse Street Festival** in Elmsbüttel, followed later in May by the **Stadtfest St Georg**.

Hamburg Pride

Hamburg's pride **shindig** (Christopher Street Day; www.hamburg-pride.de) runs over a week in late July and/or early August, with plenty of musical events, parades and a festive sense of celebration in St Georg.

MS Dockville

This wild **music festival** (www.msdockville.de/festival) takes over Wilhelmsburg on the south bank of the Elbe in mid-August with a heady mix of more than a hundred well-known and up-and-coming musicians from Germany and further afield. Works by emerging artists are also exhibited.

Hamburg Filmfest

Hamburg's annual October **film festival** (www.filmfesthamburg.de; ⊘Oct) runs over 10 days in early October screening everything from arthouse to documentary films.

Christmas Markets

From late November, numerous Christmas markets spring up all over the city. It's difficult to miss them, with examples on the Jungfernstieg waterfront, Altstadt, Hamburg and St Pauli.

Thalia Bücher
BOOKS

23 🔒 MAP P46, D3

One of Hamburg's largest bookshops, this branch of Thalia has a large selection of English-language books. It's inside the Europa Passage shopping centre. (📞040-3095 4980; www.thalia.de; Ballindamm 40, 1st fl, Europa Passage; ⊘10am-8pm Mon-Sat)

Explore ⊕
Neustadt

When the sun's out in Hamburg, there are few finer places to spend your time than Neustadt. With a front-row seat to the city's grand old waterfront buildings, Jungfernstieg is the place to fall in love with the city. Neustadt is primarily a daytime neighbourhood, with terrific shopping, a handful of interesting sights and numerous places to enjoy a good meal.

Begin your exploration by the water's edge at Jungfernstieg, overlooking Binnenalster. Spend the morning moving through the splendid arcades and canalside promenades, either window-shopping for luxury brands and watching the beautiful people glide by. Leave the crowds and explore Neustadt's west, taking in the boutiques and restaurants of Wexstrasse and Grossneumarkt (p61). While here, visit two music-themed museums, Johannes Brahms Museum (p61) and the Komponisten-Quartier (p61). Evening performances at the Staatsoper (p68) and Laeiszhalle (p69) are well worth planning your night around. It's also worth one last pass by the waterfront to enjoy Hamburg's grandeur, this time when floodlit.

Getting There & Around
Getting to and around Neustadt is often easily accomplished on foot.

U & S There are a handful of useful U-Bahn and S-Bahn stations in Neustadt, most conveniently Jungfernstieg (lines S1, S2, S3, U1, U2 and U3) with its connections across the city. Other useful stations are Gänsemarkt (line U2), Stadthausbrücke (S1, S2 and S3) and Rödingsmarkt (U3).

Neustadt Map on p62

Jungfernstieg (p65) BILDAGENTUR-ONLINE/JOKO/ALAMY ©

Top Sights 📷
St Michaelis Kirche

'Der Michel', as it is affectionately called by its friends, is one of Hamburg's most recognisable landmarks and northern Germany's largest Protestant baroque church – the Church of St Michael dominates the skyline for miles around. Ascending the tower (by steps or lift) rewards visitors with great panoramas across the city and canals. The church itself is also worth exploring.

◎ **MAP P62, A4**

www.st-michaelis.de

Englische Planke 1

tower adult/child €5/3.50, crypt €4/2.50, combo ticket €7/4, church only €2

⊘ 9am-7.30pm May-Oct, 10am-5.30pm Nov-Apr

Ⓤ Rödingsmarkt

Architecture & History

Hamburg's largest church is the third church on this site, and what you see today is an early-20th-century replica of the two previous versions, which were destroyed by fire. The church's steeple stands 132m high and has historically been used for orientation by ships sailing down the Elbe.

The Tower

The energetic among you will want to climb to the viewing platform 83m above street level, but there is also a lift that takes you up there in no time. The views are simply wonderful and it's worth spending as long as you can to pick out Hamburg's canals, waterways and other landmarks. The views towards the harbour are particularly memorable, especially with the Elbphilharmonie in all its glory.

The Sanctuary

There are prettier church interiors in Germany and, truth be told, the church's main sanctuary is cavernous and quite unadorned, as is the Protestant way. But what we really love about it is the sheer scale. There's room in here for 2500 seats, and the Latin cross plan is a classic cathedral layout. There are also an astonishing five organs.

The Crypt

Even though it costs extra, don't forego the rather crowded crypt, where nearly 2500 luminaries are buried, including composer Carl Philipp Emanuel Bach (son of the more famous Johann). The crypt, which was restored at the turn of the century, was used as an air-raid shelter during WWII. These days it hosts church services (the church's dwindling congregation gets rather lost upstairs) and concerts, and has an engaging multimedia exhibit on the city's history.

★ Top Tips

o If you're here to climb the tower and don't want to wait around, get here at opening time, as bus tours roll in soon thereafter.

o Late in the day is best for photographers – the best views of the city from the tower are late in the afternoon when the light turns Hamburg a magical golden colour.

o Check the weather forecast before visiting – it seems obvious, but it can be pretty miserable up there if it's cold and wet.

✕ Take a Break

If it's a sit-down meal you're after, exit the church's main door and cross the street to Old Commercial Room (p65), good for traditional Hamburg dishes.

A five- to 10-minute walk to the north will take you to Grossneumarkt and Thämer's (p61), a terrific neighbourhood pub with decent food.

Walking Tour 🥾

Neustadt's West

Anyone can shop and admire the arcades and luxury brands by the water in Neustadt. For something a little different, and to really hear the heartbeat of the neighbourhood, head out west to Wextrasse and around, where you'll find neighbourhood life quietly going about its business, with some fine, home-grown musical offerings thrown in.

Walk Facts

Start Johannes Brahms Museum; **S** Stadthausbrücke, **U** St Pauli

End Anne Zimmer; **S** Stadthausbrücke

Length 450m

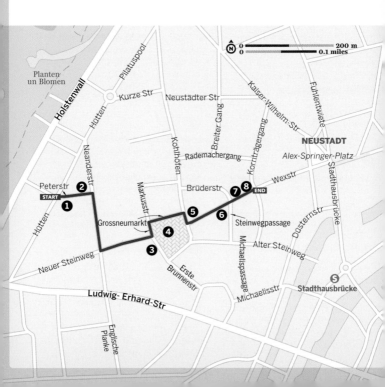

❶ Johannes Brahms Museum

Master composer Johannes Brahms (1833-97) was born in Hamburg. Although the house where he was born was destroyed in 1943, this fine 18th-century **building** (📞040-4191 3086; www. brahms-hamburg.de; Peterstrasse 39; adult/child €5/free, combined ticket with Komponisten-Quartier €7; ⏰10am-5pm Tue-Sun) is an excellent substitute. All manner of original Brahms memorabilia is on display.

❷ Komponisten-Quartier

This engaging **museum** (📞040-636 078 82; www.komponistenquartier. de; Peterstrasse 29-39; adult/child €5/free; ⏰10am-5pm Tue-Sun) celebrates the classical composers with a significant connection to the city, among them Felix Mendelssohn, Gustav Mahler and Carl Philipp Emanuel Bach.

❸ Pelikan Apotheke

This still-functioning **pharmacy** (Grossneumarkt 37; ⏰8.30am-6.30pm Mon-Fri, to 1pm Sat) has been around since 1656... wander in to admire the splendid period touches.

❹ Grossneumarkt

Once the hub of Neustadt life, this large, leafy square is pretty quiet these days, although it comes to life with market stalls on Wednesday and Saturday (8.30am-1.30pm); the food trucks that turn up are almost worth the trip alone.

❺ Thämer's

The leafy Grossneumarkt is a relaxed change from the more chichi parts of Neustadt, and for decades **Thämer's** (📞040-345 077; www.thae-mers.de; Grossneumarkt 10; mains €8-19; ⏰noon-midnight;) has anchored a prime spot on the square. Hearty German meals plus burgers are the speciality; the beer list is tops.

❻ Zum Spätzle

Specialising in *Spätzle* (a pasta-like dish from Schwabia) and *Maultaschen* (a filled pasta, also from further south), **Zum Spätzle** (📞040-3573 9516; www.zumspaetzle. de; Wexstrasse 31; mains from €8.90; ⏰noon-10pm) is a terrific place to sample German regional cuisine. We love it for its home cooking and the calm intimacy of its dining room.

❼ Public Coffee Roasters

Lovers of fine coffee consider it worth crossing town to enjoy the quiet, casual atmosphere and selection of excellent coffees straight from the **roastery** (www.public coffeeroasters.com; Wexstrasse 28; ⏰8.30am-6pm Mon-Fri, 10.30am-5pm Sat & Sun; Ⓢ Stadthausbrücke).

❽ Anne Zimmer

This gorgeous little **boutique** (📞040-5577 5447; www.annezimmer. de; Wexstrasse 28; ⏰11am-7pm Tue-Fri, to 4pm Sat) selling handmade jewellery and homewares is a lovely counterpoint to the luxury international brands that dominate Neustadt elsewhere.

A **B** **C** **D**

Dammtor

Alsterglacis

Planten un Blomen

Stephansplatz

Stephansplatz

1

Holstenglacis

Jungiusstr

Karolinenstr

Messehallen

Kleine Wallanlagen

Gorch-Fock-Wall

Esplanade

Dammtorwall

Stephansplatz

10

16

2

15

Drehbahn

Grosse Theaterstr

23

Dammtorstr

2

Galerie Herold

18

Neuer Jungfernstieg

Colonnaden

Johannes Brahms Platz

20

Gänsemarkt

Dragonerstall

Valentinskamp

Gänsemarkt

Binnenalster

Planten un Blomen

22

Jungfernstieg

Hamburg City Tours

6

14

Kaiser-Wilhelm-Str

Fuhlentwiete

ABC Str

Hohe Bleichen

21

ATG Alster-Touristik

7

Holstenwall

Platuspool

Neustädter Str

13

Hanseviertel

25

Poststr

Jungfernstieg

Hütten

Grosse Bleichen

Bleichenfleet

Alsterarkaden

3

3

NEUSTADT

Bleichenbrücke

Adolfsbrücke

Rathausmarkt

Rathaus

17

11

Wexstr

Neanderstr

Grossneumarkt

24

19

Alter Steinweg

Stadthausbrücke

Gänsekeller

Alter Wall

ALTSTADT

4

Neuer Wall

Börsenbrücke

St Michaelis Kirche

Ludwig-Erhard-Str

Rödingsmarkt

Grosser Burstah

Trostbrücke

Englische Planke

9

1

Krayenkamp

Krameramtswohnungen

Böhmkenstr

Venusberg

8

Ditmar-Koel-Str

Neuer Neustädter Weg

Rambachstr

Stubbenhuk

Herrengraben

Alsterfleet

Rödingsmarkt

Deichstr

5

12

Rambachstr

Schaartor

Baumwall

Kajen

Baumwall

5

Barkassen-Centrale Ehlers

For reviews see	
⬤ Top Sights	p58
◉ Sights	p63
✕ Eating	p65
🍷 Drinking	p68
✪ Entertainment	p68
🛍 Shopping	p69

SPEICHERSTADT

6

Cap San Diego

4

N 0 ___ 400 m
0 ___ 0.2 miles

A **B** **C** **D**

Sights

The Neustadt blends seamlessly with the Altstadt in the posh surrounds of the Binnenalster. The mood is set by the Alsterarkaden (p64) with its elegant arcades of boutiques and eateries beside the Alsterfleet canal. Away from the water, A-list attractions are rare and far flung, although there are a couple of focal points, from St Michaelis Kirche (p58) in the south, close to the port area, Grossneumarkt (p61) out west, and the fine classical music museums nearby.

Krameramtswohnungen

HISTORIC BUILDING

1 MAP P62, B4

In an alley off Krayenkamp 10 are the Krameramtswohnungen, a row of tiny half-timbered houses from the 17th century that, for nearly 200 years, were almshouses for the widows of members of the Guild of Small Shopkeepers. Today they house shops and restaurants, plus a little summer-only museum relating to the buildings. (Krayenkamp 10; S Stadthausbrücke)

Galerie Herold

GALLERY

2 MAP P62, D2

This small but rewarding private gallery is worth a look if you're in the area. Its focus is on northern German expressionism. (✆040-478 060; www.galerie-herold.de; Colonnaden 5; ⊙11am-6pm Tue-Fri; U Stephansplatz, Jungfernstieg, S Jungfernstieg)

Neustadt Sights

Krameramtswohnungen

Alsterarkaden HISTORIC BUILDING

3 MAP P62, D3

The elegant Renaissance-style arcades of the Alsterarkaden shelter upscale shops and cafes alongside the Alsterfleet canal. This is ground zero for Hamburg's ladies who lunch. (off Poststrasse; [S] Jungfernstieg)

Cap San Diego HISTORIC SITE

4 MAP P62, A6

A beautiful 1961 freighter, the 10,000-tonne *Cap San Diego* is open to tours that give a good feel for when sea voyages were a relaxing and low-key way to tour the world. There are also special exhibitions. ([☎]040-364 209; www.capsandiego.de; 3 Baumwall; adult/child €7/2.50; [🕑]10am-6pm; [U]Baumwall)

Barkassen-Centrale Ehlers BOATING

5 MAP P62, B6

Offers the usual one-hour harbour tour, but also runs a fascinating two-hour tour of the harbour, as well as canal tours and specialised trips in historic boats. ([☎]040-319 916 170; www.barkassen-centrale.de; Vorsetzen-Angleger; tours from adult/child €20/10; [U]Baumwall)

Hamburg City Tours TOURS

6 MAP P62, D3

Take a ride around the lake on Germany's oldest functioning steam boat, the *St Georg* (1876). Departures are from Jungfernstieg's pier up to four times daily. ([☎]040-181 300 410; adult/child €14/free; [🕑]Mar-Oct; [U]Jungfernstieg, [S]Jungfernstieg)

Binnenalster lake

ATG Alster-Touristik

BOATING

7 MAP P62, D3

Runs a hop-on, hop-off service between nine landing stages around the lakes. There are a lot of other tours on offer – especially interesting are the canal tours. Most only run in summer, but there's a Winter Warmer tour during the colder months. (📞040-3574 2419; www.alstertouristik.de; Jungfernstieg pier; tours adult/child from €15/7.50; 🕑Apr-Oct; Ⓢ Jungfernstieg)

Eating

True to its refined personality, Neustadt is dominated by high-end restaurants, including some of the city's most celebrated tables. Look for luxe cafes under the beautiful columned arcades of the Alsterarkaden (p64) and the appropriately named Colonnaden.

But away from the waterfront, there are plenty of more reasonably priced options, with particularly rich pickings along Colonnaden (west of Binnenalster) and, even more so, along Wexstrasse, out in Neustadt's far west; the latter has some stunning little options that are utterly unpretentious. Food trucks are a feature of the Wednesday market at Grossneumarkt (p61).

Cafe Sul

CAFE €

8 MAP P62, A5

A perfect place of refuge from the fried-fish-clutching mobs of the

What's in a Name? 👍

The **Binnenalster** (or Inner Alster Lake) waterfront, known as **Jungfernstieg**, is such a fixture of Hamburg's Neustadt that many locals don't even know the origin for the name. In ancient times, families used to bring their unmarried daughters (*jungfern*) to the promenade for a stroll.

port area, this cafe lives up to its name with a cheery disposition, even on a cloudy day. The front opens to the street and there are excellent breakfast and tapas menus. (📞040-3179 7486; www.cafe-sul.de; Ditmar-Koel-Strasse 10; mains €4-9; 🕑8am-midnight; Ⓤ Baurnwall)

Old Commercial Room

GERMAN €€

9 MAP P62, A4

Around since 1795 and opposite the entrance to St Michaelis Kirche, this fine old bastion of tradition has long been serving some of Hamburg's best *Labskaus* (a meat, fish and potato stew). Yes, it's touristy and they certainly don't mind name-dropping all of the international celebrities that have visited here. But the food is excellent. (📞040-366 319; www.oldcommercialroom.de; Englische Planke 10; mains €13-35; 🕑noon-midnight; Ⓤ Rödingsmarkt)

Johannes Brahms

If Hamburg's musical establishment had to identify their most beloved musical identity, there's a fair chance that most of them would choose Johannes Brahms (1833–1897). Born in Hamburg and baptised in the St Michaelis Kirche, Brahms would go on to become one of classical music's so-called 'three B's' – Bach, Beethoven and Brahms.

The young Johannes came from fine musical stock – his father had first arrived in Hamburg as a bit-part musician, and went on to play double bass for the Hamburg Stadttheater and the Hamburg Philharmonic Society. Brahms played in his first concert at age 10, and composed his first piece, a piano sonata in G minor, just two years later.

Brahms' reception in the city of his birth wasn't always a success. He was turned down for the role of conductor of the Hamburg Philharmonic in 1862, a position he longed for but never gained – by the time it was offered to him 30 years later, he turned it down due to other commitments. He was both friend and contemporary of the renowned composers Antonín Dvořák, Gustav Mahler and Johan Strauss II, and he spent much of his professional life in Vienna.

His magnificent body of work has many highlights, including all of his symphonies and his much-loved *Piano Concerto No. 2*. In all, he composed two serenades, four symphonies, two piano concertos (*No. 1* in D minor; *No. 2* in B-flat major), a violin concerto, and a concerto for violin and cello, as well as a large body of chamber and choral music. Of the latter, *A German Requiem* is considered among his finest works. Sadly many of his earlier works were lost – Brahms was such a perfectionist that he destroyed most of his early compositions.

In 1889, eight years before his death from cancer, Hamburg named Brahms an honorary citizen of the city.

Hamburger Fischerstube

GERMAN €€

10 ✖ MAP P62, D2

Like any port city worthy of its fishing fleet, Hamburgers have an abiding love for fish dishes, and this old-fashioned, no-frills purveyor of local dishes is a good chance to get a taste of it. Fish, lightly battered or grilled, and the house potato salad are the no-nonsense highlights. (040-3571 6380; Colonnaden 49; mains €11-23; ⏰11am-midnight; Ⓤ Stephansplatz)

Trattoria Da Enzo

ITALIAN €€

11 ✖ MAP P62, B4

Checked tablecloths, wooden chairs and down-home Italian cooking make this one of the city's more intimate Mediterranean choices. In addition to the perfectly prepared pasta, we loved the antipasti, salads and carpaccio (yes, we did visit more than once...). Fish lovers should order the turbot. No question. (☎040-3571 3366; www.trattoria-enzo.de; Wexstrasse 34; mains €11-23; ☻noon-3pm & 6-11.30pm Mon-Fri, 6-11.30pm Sat; Ⓢ Stadthausbrücke)

Lusitano

PORTUGUESE €€

12 ⊗ MAP P62, A6

As unadorned as a piece of salt cod, this little restaurant in Hamburg's old Portuguese neighbourhood captures the bright flavours of the Mediterranean. Dishes like spicy sausages and pasta will warm your heart, but the seafood is the real star. Order the Gambas James Brown and be prepared for feel-good garlicky prawns as vola-

tile as the namesake singer. Book ahead. (☎040-315 841; Rambachstrasse 5; mains €8-20; ☻noon-11pm; Ⓤ Baurnwall)

Die Bank

BRASSERIE €€€

13 ⊗ MAP P62, C3

Inhabiting the glorious *Jugendstil* (art-nouveau) interior of an 1897 bank, Die Bank is one of Hamburg's most respected kitchens and draws the great and good of the city. Head chef Thomas Fischer has won a Michelin star elsewhere, and his cooking is light, assured and creative. The menu changes with the seasons. (☎040-0238 0030; www.diebank-brasserie. de; Hohe Bleichen 17; mains €19-35, set menus from €39; ☻noon-4.30pm & 5.30-10.30pm Mon-Sat; Ⓤ Jungfernstieg, Gänsemarkt, Ⓢ Jungfernstieg)

Neustadt Eating

Johannes Brahms Museum (p61)

Marblau

MEDITERRANEAN €€€

14 🍴 MAP P62, B3

You could order a pizza here, but Marblau is known for its creative Med fusion dishes, with subtle riffs on pastas and grills. The decor is a mix of retro and contemporary, which kind of suits the whole outlook here – faithful to tradition but with one eye on the future. (📞040-226 161 555; www.marblau. de; Poolstrasse 21; mains €12-26; 🕐noon-3pm & 5pm-midnight Mon-Fri, 5-11pm Sat, 12.30-3pm & 5-11pm Sun; 🚇Gänsemarkt)

[m]eatery

STEAK €€€

15 🍴 MAP P62, C2

Tucked away on a quiet street in Neustadt's north, [m]eatery stays true to its name and prepares what many Hamburgers believe to be the best steaks in the city. Steak in all their glory dominate, but you can also get fish or salads, and even the occasional veggie dish. Ultramodern decor is very new Hamburg. (📞040-3099 9595; www.meatery.de; Drehbahn 49; mains €15-33; 🕐noon-10pm Mon-Fri, from 3pm Sat & Sun; 🚇Gänsemarkt)

Matsumi

JAPANESE €€€

16 🍴 MAP P62, D2

Celebrated sushi chef Hideaki Morita creates excellent Japanese fare at this 2nd-floor restaurant where virtually everything is unassuming, except for the food. Besides sushi, there are various teriyaki grills, a bevy of tempura dishes and *washinabe* (a stew of fish and vegetables that boils at your table). Explore the sake menu. (📞040-343 125; www.matsumi.de; Colonnaden 96; mains from €14; 🕐noon-2.30pm & 6.30-11pm Tue-Sat; 🚇Stephansplatz)

Drinking

There are many reasons to spend time in Neustadt, but nightlife is not one of them. The outdoor tables of the cafes and bars close to the waterfront tend to be over-priced and touristy, and there just aren't that many places elsewhere. There are much better options in neighbouring Altstadt and St Pauli.

Herr Buhbe

BAR

17 🍺 MAP P62, B4

Inhabiting one of Hamburg's oldest wine cellars (the wood panelling is magnificent), and the sister bar to upstairs Thämer's (p61), Herr Buhbe is a solid choice in an area of town where there aren't that many. There's plenty of beer on tap, a decent wine list of predominantly French and German wines, and a good list of mid-shelf spirits. (📞040-346 689; Wexstrasse 42; 🕐6pm-late Mon-Sat; 🚇Stadthausbrücke)

Entertainment

Staatsoper

OPERA

18 ⭐ MAP P62, C2

Among the world's most respected opera houses, the Staatsoper has been directed by the likes of Gustav Mahler and Karl Böhm during its 325-year-plus history. (📞040-356 868; www.hamburgische-staatsoper.de; Grosse Theaterstrasse 25; 🕐box office 10am-6pm Mon-Sat, plus 90min prior to performances; Ⓤ Stephansplatz)

Cotton Club JAZZ

19 ⭐ MAP P62, B4

It has moved around a lot in its time, but wherever it has been in Hamburg, the city's oldest jazz club has been reliable for live jazz in all its forms, with some blues thrown in. Gigs start at 8.30pm. (📞040-343 878; www.cotton-club.de; Alter Steinweg 10; €8; 🕐8pm-midnight Mon-Thu, to 1am Fri & Sat, 11am-2.30pm Sun; Ⓢ Stadthausbrücke)

Laeiszhalle CLASSICAL MUSIC

20 ⭐ MAP P62, B2

Built in 1908, the Laeiszhalle was Hamburg's premier address for classical concerts and opera. That mantle has passed to the extraordinary new Elbphilharmonie, but this splendid neobaroque edifice still hosts a regular calendar of classical performances. (📞040-346 920; www.elbphilharmonie.de/en/laeiszhalle; Johannes-Brahms-Platz; Ⓢ Messehallen)

Shopping

Neustadt is one of the best places in Hamburg to go shopping. In the elegant blocks south of the Binnenalster waterfront, every imaginable international luxury brand rubs shoulders with fashion

Neustadt Shopping

Die Bank (p67)

chains like Zara and H&M. Those who enjoy shopping could spend hours here. Upmarket shops are located within the triangle created by Jungfernstieg, Fuhlentwiete and Neuer Wall.

In addition to fashion, Neustadt also boasts two of Hamburg's best sellers of wines and local food products. In the neighbourhood's west, particularly around Wexstrasse, look out for little boutiques selling artisan jewellery and homewares. The twice-weekly market at Grossneumarkt (p61) is also a fine affair.

Mutterland
FOOD & DRINKS

21 🔒 MAP P62, C3

This 'Made in Germany' delicatessen has beautifully packaged and utterly tempting foods (jams,

chocolates etc) and drinks (try the Monkey 47 Schwarzwald Dry Gin, from the Black Forest). It's a stunning collection and it's very difficult to leave without spending large amounts of money. (📞040-3500 4360; www.mutterland.de; Poststrasse 14-16; ⏰8am-8pm Mon-Fri, from 9am Sat; Ⓤ Jungfernstieg, Ⓢ Jungfernstieg)

Geigenbau Winterling
MUSICAL INSTRUMENTS

22 🔒 MAP P62, B2

In a city with such a distinguished classical music tradition, Geigenbau Winterling should be a pilgrimage place for serious musicians. You'll find exquisite stringed instruments, including some extraordinary historic pieces

Staatsoper (p68)

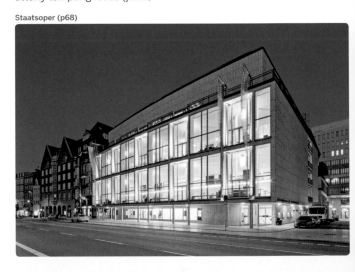

which have been restored here. It's not for the casual visitor and prices are suitably steep. But it has been an essential part of the city's musical fabric since 1890. (📞040-352 904; www.geigenbau-winterling.de; Valentinskamp 34; 🕙10am-6.30pm Tue-Fri; Ⓤ Gänsemarkt)

Apropos the Concept Store
FASHION & ACCESSORIES

23 🔒 MAP P62, D2

Perfectly at home next to the palatial **Fairmont Vier Jahreseiten Hamburg** (📞040-3494 3151; www. hvj.de; Neuer Jungfernstieg 9-14; r from €285; ❄️🛜🏊; Ⓤ Stephansplatz), this luxury concept store pulls a fine portfolio of five-star brands – including Gucci, Manolo Blahnik and Valentino – together under one roof. The surrounds are as upmarket as the accessories themselves. (📞040-280 087 750; www.apropos-store.com; Neuer Jungfernstieg 16; 🕙10am-7pm Mon-Sat; Ⓤ Stephansplatz)

Tobias Strauch Weinkontor
WINE

24 🔒 MAP P62, B4

Well-known Hamburg culinary celebrity Tobias Strauch knows what he's talking about when it comes to wine. His carefully chosen selection of mostly European wines is one of the best you'll find. (📞040-226 161 544; www.tobias-strauch.de; Wexstrasse 35; 🕙noon-8pm Mon-Fri, 11am-6pm Sat; Ⓢ Stadthausbrücke)

Hanse CD Im Hanse Viertel
MUSIC

25 🔒 MAP P62, C3

Not for music streamers: this exquisite little shop huddled amid some very posh brethren sells predominantly classical and jazz CDs and DVDs with rare and hard-to-find music and film. (📞040-340 561; www.hanse-cd.de; Grosse Bleichen 36; 🕙10am-7pm Mon-Fri, to 4pm Sat; Ⓤ Jungfernstieg, Ⓢ Jungfernstieg)

Explore
St Georg

St Georg is Hamburg in microcosm. Along its main thoroughfare, Lange Reihe, you'll find fab restaurants, bars and a real buzz, much of which comes from the city's vibrant gay community. In the neighbourhood's southern end, it's notably more seedy. And everywhere you look, Hamburg's increasingly multicultural population is changing the face of St Georg.

Begin your exploration of St Georg at the Museum für Kunst und Gewerbe (p77), the neighbourhood's major sight and conveniently on the way in from the rest of the city. After that, it's along Lange Reihe that you'll want to spend most of your time. Although there's little in the way of traditional sights, there's a real buzz about this thoroughfare, rich as it is in restaurants, bars, cafes and shopping boutiques. From Lange Reihe, quieter streets head north to Aussenalster, on the lakeside. To get a taste of St Georg, you probably won't need more than half a day.

Getting There & Around

Just about everywhere in St Georg is within easy walking distance of the Hauptbahnhof; hotels and hostels are mostly clustered at the station (southwestern) end of the neighbourhood.

U If you're coming via the subway, Hauptbahnhof-Süd (lines U1 and U3) and Hauptbahnhof-Nord (U2 and U4) are the most convenient stations.

St Georg Map on p76

Lange Reihe ULLSTEIN BILD /GETTY IMAGES ©

Walking Tour 🥾

St Georg: Alternative & Artsy

St Georg is a window on inner-urban Hamburg. At once newly multicultural and the heart of the city's gay scene, it's a sometimes gritty, offbeat neighbourhood. Its centrepiece is Lange Reihe: so much of what's good about St Georg happens along this street or not far away. Running through it all like a thread is a real sense of community.

Walk Facts

Start Hansaplatz;
Ⓤ Hauptbahnhof-Nord

End Bar M&V;
Ⓤ Hauptbahnhof-Nord

Length 1km

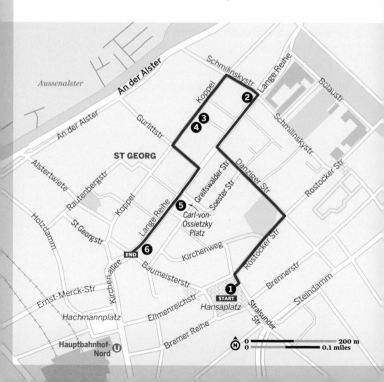

❶ Hansaplatz

The general gentrification of St Georg has even affected its somewhat seedy central square, the Hansaplatz. Completely renovated in 2011 and fully pedestrianised, the square's centrepiece is its fountain. Completed in 1878, it shows important figures in Hamburg's past, including Emperor Constantine the Great and Charlemagne, and is surmounted by a figure showing the might of the Hanseatic League.

❷ Café Gnosa

With its abstract art and in-house bakery, **Café Gnosa** (☏040-243 034; www.gnosa.de; Lange Reihe 93; mains €7-14; ⏰10am-1am) draws an affable gay and straight crowd. The curved glass windows give it an art-deco vibe. There are outside tables, and serving breakfast until 4pm daily is precisely the kind of understanding that Hamburg's nightlife deserves. It's always busy, and deservedly so.

❸ Koppel 66

Arguably Hamburg's premier collection of art-and-craft stores, the arcade at **Koppel 66** (☏040-386 419 30; www.koppel66.de; Koppel 66; ⏰11am-6pm Mon-Fri, to 4pm Sat) has some intriguing options – from hat-makers and handmade soaps, to purveyors of handmade pens and artisan jewellers.

❹ Café Koppel

Set back from busy Lange Reihe, in the gallery Koppel 66, this veggie **cafe** (☏040-249 235; www.cafe-koppel.de; Koppel 66; mains €5-10; ⏰10am-11pm; 🍴) is a refined oasis (with a summer garden). The menu could be an ad for the fertile fields of northern Germany, as the baked goods, salads, daily soups and much more are all made with fresh seasonal ingredients.

❺ Wochenmarkt

This weekly **eco-market** (www.oeko-wochenmarkt.de/maerkte/st-georg; Carl-von-Ossietzky Platz; ⏰2-6.30pm Fri) – think organic farmers' produce – adds a little life to Friday afternoons in the heart of St Georg. It sometimes shifts to Friday morning.

❻ Bar M&V

The drinks menu is like a designer catalogue at this grand old St Georg **bar** (☏040-2800 6973; www.mvbar.de; Lange Reihe 22; ⏰5pm-2am), which has been beautifully restored. Settle into one of the wooden booths, smell the freesias and enjoy the merry mixed crowd that's like a cross-section of St Georg society.

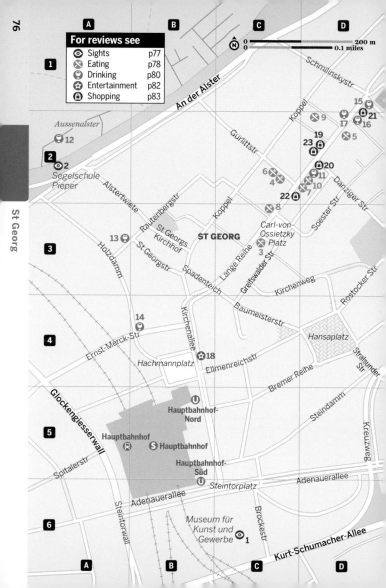

St George

For reviews see

👁	Sights	p77
✕	Eating	p78
✕	Drinking	p80
★	Entertainment	p82
🔒	Shopping	p83

An der Alster

Schmilinskystr

Aussenalster

👁 12

🔒 2

Segelschule
Pieper

Alsterwiete

Gurlittstr

Koppel

✕ 9

17 🔒 16
15
21

✕ 5

19
23 🔒

6 ✕
4 ✕

Rautenbergstr

Koppel

🔒 20
11 🔒
10
7
22 🔒

Danziger Str

✕ 8

Soester Str

Holzdamm

St Georgs
Kirchhof

St Georgstr

13 🔒

Spadenteich

ST GEORG

Lange Reihe

Carl-von-
Ossietzky
Platz

✕ 3

Greifswalder Str

Kirchenweg

Rostocker Str

Kirchenallee

Baumeisterstr

Ernst-Merck-Str

14 🔒

Hansaplatz

Ellmenreichstr

Stralsunder Str

Glockengiesserwall

★ 18

Hachmannplatz

Bremer Reihe

Steindamm

Kreuzweg

Spitalerstr

Ⓤ
Hauptbahnhof-
Nord

Hauptbahnhof
🚻

Ⓢ Hauptbahnhof

Hauptbahnhof-
Süd
Ⓤ

Steintorplatz

Adenauerallee

Steintorwall

Adenauerallee

Brockestr

Museum für
Kunst und
Gewerbe 👁 1

Kurt-Schumacher-Allee

0 ——————— 200 m
0 ——————— 0.1 miles

Sights

St Georg is more about experiences – eating, drinking and shopping in particular – than sights. Beyond these experiences, the main (some would say only) attraction is the Museum für Kunst und Gewerbe. A walk along the shore of the Aussenalster lake is a pleasant stroll.

Museum für Kunst und Gewerbe
MUSEUM

1 ◎ MAP P76, C6

The Museum für Kunst und Gewerbe is lots of fun. Its vast collection of sculpture, furniture, fashion, jewellery, posters, porcelain, musical instruments and household objects runs the gamut from Italian to Islamic, Japanese to Viennese and medieval to pop art, and includes an art-nouveau salon from the 1900 Paris World Fair. The museum cafe is part of the exhibition space. (Museum for Art & Trade; 📞040-428 542 732; www.mkg-hamburg.de; Steintorplatz 1; adult/child €12/free, after 5pm Thu €10; 🕙10am-6pm Tue-Sun, to 9pm Thu; Ⓤ Hauptbahnhof-Süd)

Segelschule Pieper
BOATING

2 ◎ MAP P76, A2

Hire your own boat for rowing or paddling (sailing requires a certificate). The calm on the water amidst the city and the views are a delight. (📞040-247 578; www.segelschule-pieper.de; An der Alster; 🕙10am-9pm Apr–mid-Oct; Ⓤ Hauptbahnhof-Nord)

Museum für Kunst und Gewerbe

Eating

St Georg is one of Hamburg's culinary hotspots to watch. All along Lange Reihe, old-school German eating houses rub shoulders with cool cafes, French and Italian bistros, and some of Hamburg's best burgers.

Otto's Burger

BURGERS €

3 ❌ MAP P76, C3

Eight different burger types, including one with truffle mayo and two veggie options, washed down by craft beers – need we say more? (📞040-2395 3382; www. ottosburger.com; Lange Reihe 40; mains from €8; ⏱11.30am-10.30pm Mon-Thu, to 11pm Fri & Sat, to 10pm Sun; Ⓤ Hauptbahnhof-Nord)

Peaberries

CAFE €

4 ❌ MAP P76, C2

Perfect for that much-needed pause, this cute little cafe has excellent coffee drinks as well as tasty baked goods, including the best bagels in town. (📞040-2419 2862; www.peaberries-kaffeeroesterei. com; Gurlittstrasse 46; mains from €3; ⏱7am-6pm Mon-Fri, 9am-4pm Sat; Ⓤ Hauptbahnhof-Nord)

Casa di Roma

ITALIAN €€

5 ❌ MAP P76, D2

One of the better and classier Italian restaurants among many in St Georg, Casa di Roma is cool, contemporary and has well-priced pasta dishes. The other meat or fish main dishes are

Market in Hansaplatz (p75)

TORSTEN KRÖGER/ALAMY ©

much pricier but well worth every euro – although the menu changes regularly, we enjoyed the grilled wolf fish fillet on creamy savoy cabbage and mashed potatoes. (📞040-280 3043; www.casadiroma. de; Lange Reihe 76; pasta €9-18, other mains €22-33; 🕐11.30am-midnight; 🚇Hauptbahnhof-Nord)

Cafe Gitane
CAFE €€

6 🗺 MAP P76, C2

We love the tasteful retro furnishings at this appealing cafe and wine bar. The small but carefully chosen menu changes with the seasons, but ranges from the Mediterranean to the North Sea. A fine list of wines, too. (📞0172 524 0747; www.cafe-gitane.com; Gurlittstrasse 44; mains €11.50-23; 🕐5-11pm Mon-Sat; 🚇Hauptbahnhof-Nord)

Central
INTERNATIONAL €€

7 🗺 MAP P76, D2

We think this place is a touch overpriced for dinner, but the international cooking (which leans predominantly in the direction of Italy) is assured, and the dishes rise above the usual Italian fare – try the squid-ink spaghetti. Service is slightly formal, especially in the evenings. Dress nice. (📞040-2805 3704; www.central-hamburg.de; Lange Reihe 50, St Georg; lunch mains €9-13, dinner mains €15-24; 🕐11am-3pm & 5-11pm Mon-Fri, 5-11pm Sat & Sun; 🚇Hauptbahnhof-Nord)

The Gentrification of St Georg

This neighbourhood, made up of large 19th-century apartment blocks for Hamburg's upper-middle classes, hit a nadir in the 1970s when thoughtless postwar reconstruction combined with a massive influx of drug dealing and prostitution to give it a very sleazy reputation.

Things are much gentrified now (look out for the great shops and cafes), and the facelift has even affected St Georg's central square, the Hansaplatz (p75).

Das Dorf
GERMAN €€€

8 🗺 MAP P76, C3

There are lots of reasons to visit this wonderfully traditional restaurant with its wood-panelled dining room. But we love it especially for its homemade bread and *Labskaus* (a stew of meat, fish and potato). It's not always on the menu in summer, but when it is, it consistently ranks among the best in Hamburg. (📞040-458 119; www. restaurant-dorf.de; Lange Reihe 39; mains €20-24; 🕐noon-11pm Mon-Fri, from 5pm Sat; 🚇Hauptbahnhof-Nord)

Le Bon Brasserie St Georg
FRENCH €€€

9 🗺 MAP P76, D2

This gem in the heart of St Georg takes French classics and messes

Worth a Trip: English Theatre of Hamburg

Germany's oldest professional English-language **theatre** (☏040-227 7089; www.englishtheatre.de; Lerchenfeld 14; tickets from €18; Ⓤ Mundsberg) has been around since 1976 and performs quality English drama with English actors to a predominantly German audience. To get here take the U-bahn or busses 25, 172, or 173 to Mundsburg.

with them as little as possible – think bouillabaisse, coq au vin or boeuf Bourguignon. With French wines and Belgian beer, it's hard to think of a better French experience in the city. The entrance is signposted on Lange Reihe. (☏040-3573 5166; www.mon-le-bon.de; Koppel 76, entry via Lange Reihe 87; mains €14.50-27; ⏱5-11pm Tue-Sun; Ⓤ Hauptbahnhof-Nord)

Cox   MODERN EUROPEAN €€€

10 🍴 MAP P76, D2

Behind its opaque glass doors, this upmarket bistro with fluted columns and period decor was part of the original vanguard of St Georg's gentrification. Its changing menu of dishes reflects seasonal foods and influences from across the continent. (☏040-249 422; www.restaurant-cox.de; Lange Reihe 68; mains lunch €10-18, dinner €17-26;

⏱noon-2.30pm & 6.30-10.30pm Mon-Fri, 6.30-10.30pm Sat & Sun; Ⓤ Hauptbahnhof-Nord)

Drinking

St Georg does late nights as well as any other inner-urban Hamburg neighbourhood, with an excellent scattering of cocktail bars, clubs and wine bars. The special St Georg twist is that most are either gay-friendly or predominantly gay. There are fine places all across the neighbourhood, but as with most things in St Georg, the richest pickings are along Lange Reihe.

Bacaro Wine Bar   WINE BAR

11 🍷 MAP P76, D2

This classy little wine bar has a contemporary feel and is ideal for an evening spent in serious conversation over Italian wine. The food, too, is excellent, making it a great place to start the night. (☏040-3570 6829; www.bacaro-winebar.de; Lange Reihe 68-70; ⏱noon-3pm & 5.30-11pm Mon-Thu, to midnight Fri, 5pm-midnight Sat, 5-11pm Sun; Ⓤ Hauptbahnhof-Nord)

a.mora   BAR

12 🍷 MAP P76, A2

Perched on the jetty overlooking Aussenalster, this suave bar is as good for breakfast or a coffee as it is for a late-night cocktail. It attracts a fairly stylish crowd, and the reclining day beds right by the water are rarely relinquished on a summer's day. It's not the most adventurous cocktail list, but why mess with the classics? (📞040-2805 6735; www.a-mora.com; An der Alster 72; ⏰10am-late; Ⓤ Hauptbahnhof-Nord)

Bar Hamburg COCKTAIL BAR

13 🚇 MAP P76, A3

A favourite haunt of A-list celebrities (Mick Jagger and Claudia Schiffer have both passed through its doors), Bar Hamburg has more than 70 different whiskies, around 250 cocktails to choose from, and a cigar and shisha zone. Music is downtempo and chilled, the seats are leather, and you should dress to impress. (📞040-2805 4880; www.barhh.com; Rautenbergstrasse 6-8; ⏰4pm-1am Sun-Thu, to 3am Fri & Sat; Ⓤ Hauptbahnhof-Nord)

Golden Cut Club CLUB

14 🚇 MAP P76, B4

One of Hamburg's top clubs, Golden Cut has a pretty strict door policy and lines can be long. The stage acts can be wild and some of the best DJs in town and touring turn up here – think house, R&B, hip-hop and big-show after-parties. (📞040-8510 3532; www.goldencut.org; Holzdamm 61; entry from €20; ⏰11pm-6am Fri & Sat; Ⓤ Hauptbahnhof-Nord)

Frau Möller BAR

15 🚇 MAP P76, D1

It's 2am Saturday and you can't live without a pork steak? Head to this St Georg institution where outside tables wrap around the corner location and the kitchen

St Georg Drinking

Café Gnosa (p75)

INGOLF POMPE/LOOK FOTO/GETTY IMAGES ©

stays open late. Besides good German standards, the wine and beer lists are the best you'll find at 5am. (☎040-2532 8817; www.fraumoeller.com; Lange Reihe 96; ⏱11am-4am Mon-Thu, to 6am Fri & Sat, to 3am Sun, kitchen 11am-3am daily; Ⓤ Hauptbahnhof-Nord)

Kyti Voo   BAR

16 🚇 MAP P76, D2

A mixed crowd mixes it up with an especially rewarding menu of craft beer and cocktails until *very* late. At sunnier (or less dark) times, grab a table on the outdoor terrace. Cocktail happy hour is a particularly generous 5pm to 8pm daily. (☎040-2805 5565; www.kytivoo.com; Lange Reihe 82; ⏱5pm-late Mon-Sat, from 2pm Sun; Ⓤ Hauptbahnhof-Nord)

Generation Bar   GAY

17 🍺 MAP P76, D2

A popular gay bar right in the middle of the St Georg gay strip. The red light adds to the hazy mood – this is a smokers joint. (☎040-2880 4690; www.generation-bar.de; Lange Reihe 81; ⏱4pm-2am Sun-Thu, to 4am Fri & Sat; Ⓤ Hauptbahnhof-Nord)

Entertainment

Deutsches Schauspielhaus Theatre   THEATRE

18 ⭐ MAP P76, B4

Germany's largest and most important theatre presents imaginative interpretations of the classics (Shakespeare, Goethe, Chekhov et al) alongside new works. It's

Deutsches Schauspielhaus Theatre

MG PHOTO/OHDE/ALAMY ©

one of the city's most dynamic cultural spaces. (📞040-248 713; www.schauspielhaus.de; Kirchenallee 39; Ⓤ Hauptbahnhof-Nord)

Shopping

Small boutiques selling Hamburg souvenirs, as well as shops selling stationery, hats and wine, make for a compact and diverse shopping experience in St Georg. But the main drawcard – one worth crossing Hamburg for – is Koppel 66 (p75), the city's finest gathering of arts-and-crafts boutiques and workshops.

Weinkauf St Georg   WINE

19 🔒 MAP P76, D2

This small but knowledgeable wine shop specialises in wines from Germany, France, Italy and Spain, although you might find the occasional bottle from further afield, as well as champagnes and spirits. (📞040-280 3387; www.weinkauf-st-georg.de; Lange Reihe 73; ⏱11am-7.30pm Mon-Fri, 10am-6pm Sat; Ⓤ Hauptbahnhof-Nord)

Kaufhaus Hamburg   GIFTS & SOUVENIRS

20 🔒 MAP P76, D2

Fun Hamburg-themed souvenirs make shopping for a gift back home rather enjoyable. There's everything from stationery and homewares to games and food. (📞040-2281 5669; www.kaufhaus-hamburg.de; Lange Reihe 70;

⏱11am-7pm Mon-Fri, from 10am Sat; Ⓤ Hauptbahnhof-Nord)

Chapeau St Georg   HATS

21 🔒 MAP P76, D2

Arrived in Hamburg without your hat? Fear not, because Chapeau St Georg will have your head covered in no time. These aren't headgear of the I-Love-Hamburg souvenir variety, but rather stylish toppers for special occasions, as well as more traditional brimmed hats. (📞040-2800 4375; www.chapeau-stgeorg.de; Lange Reihe 94; ⏱11am-6pm Mon-Sat; Ⓤ Hauptbahnhof-Nord)

Art of Hamburg   GIFTS & SOUVENIRS

22 🔒 MAP P76, C2

Fun clothes, bags and other accessories with nautical colours and Hamburg slogans or other references make this a good place for cheerful souvenirs from the city. (📞040-7718 0814; www.the-art-of-hamburg.de; Lange Reihe 48; ⏱11am-7pm Mon-Sat; Ⓤ Hauptbahnhof-Nord)

Blendwerk   STATIONERY

23 🔒 MAP P76, D2

Blendwerk caters to all your stationery needs, from Leuchtturm notebooks to knick-knacks for your desk you never knew you needed. (📞040-240 003; www.blendwerk-hamburg.de; Lange Reihe 73; ⏱11am-7pm Mon-Fri, to 6pm Sat; Ⓤ Hauptbahnhof-Nord)

Explore ◉

Speicherstadt & HafenCity

Welcome to the waterfront. The seven-storey red-brick warehouses lining the Speicherstadt archipelago are a famous Hamburg symbol and they're increasingly filled with fine museums. HafenCity, crowned by the superlative Elbphilharmonie, is Hamburg's most architecturally dynamic corner, with a world seemingly being created before your eyes. This vast new quarter, when fully completed, will transform the city. Then again, it already has.

Begin your morning at Elbphilharmonie (p86). Another place that rewards an early start is Miniatur Wunderland (p90), an equally popular attraction. With these two stellar sights out of the way, wander along Hamburg's golden mile of museums, picking and choosing which of the many options on offer most appeals. There are a few choices for lunch nearby. Given that HafenCity is something of a work-in-progress, visit the HafenCity InfoCenter (p93) to check what tours are available, or to pick up their booklets and maps on the area so that you can explore on your own.

Getting There & Around

Ⓤ A new underground line, the U4, links HafenCity from the Überseequartier stop to the rest of the city. Otherwise, it's a short walk from either Messberg U-Bahn station (line U1) or Baumwall (line U3). Alternatively, Speicherstadt and HafenCity are an easy 10-minute walk south of the city centre.

Speicherstadt & HafenCity Map on p94

Speicherstadt warehouses NIK WALLER PRODUCTIONS/SHUTTERSTOCK ©

Top Sights 📸
Elbphilharmonie

It is rare that a building comes along with so much hype and so much controversy, only for a collective gasp of excitement to be heard upon its completion. Elbphilharmonie (Elbe Philharmonic Hall or 'Elphi' to its friends) is one such building. Whether you're looking at it from afar or watching a concert within, there is one near-universal response: Wow!

◉ MAP P94, A3
📞 040-3576 6666
www.elbphilharmonie.de
Platz der Deutschen Einheit 4
admission free
🕐 9am-11.30pm
Ⓢ Baumwall

The Entrance

From street level, the 82m-long escalator is the first sign that the interior is every bit as special as the world-famous facade. Said to be the longest escalator in Europe, it's a long, slightly curved golden tube, like traversing a tunnel of magical bubbles.

The Plaza

Atop the escalators, and negotiated via a series of Escher-like stairways, the Plaza has a shop, restaurants and the hotel entrance. But head for the balcony or viewing platform that wraps around the entire structure. There are splendid views to be had at every turn.

Concert Hall

The building is one thing, but its raison d'être – the concert hall and other performance spaces – are arguably the best in the world. Acoustically the concert hall is the most advanced in existence, and with specially tiered seating to enhance the connection between audience and performer, the Grand Hall is a fabulous place to attend a concert.

Architecture & History

Elbphilharmonie arrived late and well over budget. But what a result! Essentially two buildings in one, the bottom half is a converted brick warehouse whose facade is largely unchanged; it stored cocoa, tea and tobacco until the 1990s. Sitting atop the warehouse, on its own foundations, is a soaring edifice of more than 1000 curved glass panels, evoking so many waves upon the Elbe. It was all designed by Swiss architectural firm Herzog & de Meuron.

★ Top Tips

o Entrance is free but you must take a ticket from the ticket office and scan the barcode to pass through the gates.

o Pick up the free *Elbphilharmonie Hamburg* brochure from the shop – it has a useful diagram of the building.

o If you want to attend a concert here, check the program as soon as you know you'll be travelling to Hamburg, as tickets sell out fast.

o To take an excellent photograph of Elbphilharmonie with red-brick warehouses in the foreground, head to Holzbrücke, a short distance north.

✗ Take a Break

Right across from the entrance, Carls Brasserie (p97) does French bistro snacks that are ideal for lunch.

Although there's a restaurant and cafe inside, if you want to stretch your legs, Deichstrasse is only a 15-minute walk away.

Top Sights 📷

Internationales Maritimes Museum

Hamburg is defined by its maritime past, and there's nowhere better to understand this fascinating history than the International Maritime Museum. More than that, the location, by the water in a neighbourhood where the city is once again reinventing itself with one eye cast seawards, couldn't be more appropriate. Even if you're not into old ships, don't miss this one.

◎ **MAP P94, C2**

www.internationales
-maritimes-museum.de

Koreastrasse 1

adult/concession
€13/9.50

🕙10am-6pm

Ⓤ Messberg,
Überseequartier

The Big Picture

It can be worth wandering through the collection quite quickly to get an overview of the scale of what's on offer, then go back and dip into the sections that particularly interest you. Considered the world's largest private collection of maritime treasures, it includes a mind-numbing 26,000 model ships, 50,000 construction plans, 5000 illustrations, 2000 films, 1.5 million photographs and much more.

Kaispeicher B

There's something rather apt about the fact that this terrific collection inhabits what is believed to be Hamburg's oldest waterfront warehouse. Built in 1878 as a grain silo, the 10-storey warehouse, with its neo-Gothic gables and cornices, would come to represent the prevailing style in 19th-century Hamburg and the Hanseatic ports beyond. Given that there's so much new construction taking place all around, the Kaispeicher B is an important anchor to the past.

Early Maritime History

Don't miss the early stages of humankind's 3000-year fascination with the sea. Ancient navigational devices, rudimentary communication systems and models of ships belonging to everyone from the Phoenicians to the Vikings are an astonishing journey through civilisations and our need to look beyond the horizon. Don't miss the 1657 *Atlantis Majoris* from 1657, the first-ever nautical atlas, from the Netherlands.

Shipbuilding

Another must-see part of the exhibition is the mechanics of shipbuilding and how it's changed through the centuries with developments in design and technology. The story begins with dugout canoes, including a millennia-old hollowed-out tree trunk found not far from here.

★ **Top Tips**

o If you've got time, consider making a couple of visits – trying to cram 3000 years of history into one day can be a little overwhelming.

o If you're only making one visit, allow a good half-day to do justice to the extensive exhibition.

✕ **Take a Break**

A five-minute walk east of the museum, Fleetschlösschen (p97) is the perfect HafenCity bistro.

The hamburgers (the food, not the people) at Oberhafen Kantine (p93), just around the corner, are the most traditional in town.

Speicherstadt & HafenCity Internationales Maritimes Museum

Top Sights 📷
Miniatur Wunderland

Even the worst cynics are quickly transformed into fans of this vast miniature wonderland, the world's largest model railway. The model trains wending their way through all manner of European tableaux are hugely impressive. But when you see a model A380 swoop out of the sky and land at the fully functional model airport, you can't help but gasp.

◎ MAP P94, A2

☏ 040-300 6800

www.miniatur
-wunderland.de

Kehrwieder 2

adult/child €15/7.50

🕐 hours vary

Ⓤ Baumwall

Hamburg

There's no doubt in our mind that the high-light of the whole collection (apart from the airport) is the reconstruction of Hamburg, not least because of its familiarity and immediacy. Everything from the port to the church steeples is almost perfectly rendered, with trains zipping between it all. Note the impressive Millerntor-Stadion where SV Hamburger is beating St Pauli 3:0 – in Hamburg, such calculated insults are never accidental.

Europe & Beyond

The main exhibition floor also takes in Scandinavia (Narvik and Kiruna), Austria, the US (where Las Vegas segues effortlessly into Miami Beach), Middle Germany and Knuffingen – a recreated German town that is exceptionally good. As you wander between them all, don't miss the control room, a large bank of televisions that NASA would be proud of.

Knuffingen Airport

The highlight of the entire exhibition, planes take over from trains for this vast, fully functioning airport in miniature. Planes taxi, take off and land, and there's even a crashed plane, with flames, smoke and fire engines rushing to the scene. Simply mesmerising.

Best of the Rest

Follow Switzerland down the mountain, past the chocolate factory, to the floor below where all manner of European scenes are on show. Here, we particularly enjoyed Venice and Rome (complete with Trevi Fountain). Watch also for the dioramas that give a quick overview of German history; the WWII ones are riveting.

★ Top Tips

o On weekends and in summer holidays, prepurchase your ticket online to skip the queues.

o Even so, get here early to avoid having to stand behind a row of people and wait for your turn at each exhibit.

o Although you are sent first through the shop, resist the urge to buy – you also leave this way.

o Kids will enjoy the Wunderland Sweep-stakes, which asks you to track down 15 tiny details for the chance to win a prize; it's on the *Visitors Guide* given to you with your ticket.

✕ Take a Break

Deichstrasse is a five-minute walk away, across the canal. Head there for potato pancakes at Kartoffelkeller (p50).

For a meal that could be fine dining or pasta, walk a block or so east to Vlet in der Speicher-stadt (p93).

Walking Tour

Learning About the Past

Speicherstadt and HafenCity may have vastly disparate origins – the former is one of the oldest corners of Hamburg's port, the latter its newest. But one thing they share: it's only recently that Hamburgers have moved in to live here. They're still finding their way, and they're learning lots about their city in the process.

Walk Facts

Start HafenCity Info-Center; Ⓤ Messberg

End Vlet in der Speicherstadt; Ⓤ Messberg

Length 3km

❶ HafenCity InfoCenter

You can pick up brochures and check out detailed architectural models and installations that give a sense of the immensity of the HafenCity project at this **information centre** (☏040-3690 1799; www.hafencity.com; Am Sandtorkai 30; admission free; ◷10am-6pm Tue-Sun). The centre also offers a program of free guided tours through the evolving district; check the website for more information.

❷ Speicherstadt Museum

To see where Speicherstadt comes from, locals visit this **century-old warehouse** (☏040-321 191; www.speicherstadtmuseum.de; Am Sandtorkai 36; adult/child €4/2; ◷10am-5pm Mon-Fri, to 6pm Sat & Sun Mar-Nov, 10am-5pm Tue-Sun Nov-Mar), which is the atmospheric backdrop for exhibitions on Hamburg's trading past. There are sometimes demonstrations on the trade in tea or coffee; check the website for details (per person €10).

❸ HafenCity Nachhaltigkeitspavillon

For an alternative, greener take on the whole HafenCity development, this intriguing **exhibit** (Osaka 9; ☏040-3747 2660; www.hafencity.com; Osakaallee 9; admission free; ◷10am-6pm Tue-Sun) takes a look at sustainable urban development and environmentally sound construction.

❹ Oberhafen Kantine

Since 1925, this slightly tilted brick **restaurant** (☏040-3280 9984; www.oberhafenkantine-hamburg.de; Stockmeyerstrasse 39; mains €10-28; ◷noon-10pm Tue-Sat, noon-5.30pm Sun) has served up the most traditional Hamburg fare. Here you can order a 'Hamburger' and you get the real thing: a patty made with various seasonings and onions. Roast beef and fish round out a trip back to the days when the surrounding piers echoed to the shouts of seafarers.

❺ Kaffee Museum

This excellent **museum** (☏040-5520 4258; www.kaffeemuseum-burg.de; St Annenufer 2; entry & tour €10; ◷tours 10am, noon, 2pm & 4pm Tue-Sun) takes you through Hamburg's coffee trading history and has a live roasting demonstration. Try the resulting brew in the cafe. Check out the website for a range of activities that can include coffee, tea and even gin tasting.

❻ Vlet in der Speicherstadt

Right by the pedestrian bridge, **Vlet** (☏040-334 753 750; www.vlet.de; Am Sandtorkai 23-24; mains €23-38; ◷5pm-midnight Mon-Sat) has three different menus (plus a children's version) and the recurring theme is the intersection between contemporary flair and German traditional dishes, with options including *Labskaus* and *Pannfisch* (fried Arctic char). There are also some weird and wonderful starters.

Speicherstadt & HafenCity

400 m
0.2 miles

1

Bankstr

Oberhafenbrücke

Versmannstr

Baakenpark 🚶 **4**

2

3

Deichtorstr

Deichtorplatz

Oberbaumbrücke

Obermühlenbrücke

Ericusbrücke

Stockmeyerstr

Am Lohsepark

Shanghaiallee

Koreastr

✕ 5

Osakaallee

Überseequartier

Am Dalmannkai

HAFENCITY

Hübenerstr

Messberg

🚇 Messberg

Poggenmühlenbrücke

Alter Wandrahm

Brooktorkai

St Annenufer

3
HafenCity
Riverbus

6 ✕

Internationales
Maritimes
Museum

Am Sandtorpark

Grosser Grasbrook

Zippelhaus

Neuer Wandrahm

Katherinenstr

Willy-Brandt-Str

Bei den Mühren

SPEICHERSTADT

Spicy's
Gewürzmuseum

Hamburg
Dungeon

Am Sandtorkai

Kehrwieder

Am Kaiserkai

✕ 7

Sandtorhafen

ALTSTADT

🚇 Rödingsmarkt

Trostbrücke

Ludwig-Erhard-Str

Rödingstr

Kajen

Deichstr

Cremon

Hohe
Brücke

Miniatur
Wunderland

◎ 1

◎ 2

Platz der
Deutschen
Einheit

Elbphilharmonie

◎ 3
✦ 8

🚇 **E** **N**

F

A **B** **C** **D**

Sights

Elbphilharmonie might be getting all the attention at the moment, but Speicherstadt has an extraordinary concentration of museums, from the world's largest model train network and a horror-movie amusement park to museums devoted to coffee, spices, Hamburg's maritime history and and sustainable urban development. If you can't find something here to pique your curiosity, you're probably in the wrong city.

Hamburg Dungeon

AMUSEMENT PARK

1 MAP P94, B2

This camped-up chamber of horrors is brought to life by actors, incorporating various thrill rides, and is housed in an old warehouse. It's pricey and not recommended for kids under 10. (☏1806; www.thedungeons.com; Kehrwieder 2; adult/child €25.50/20; ⊙10am-6pm Jul & Aug, to 5pm Mar-Jun & Sep-Dec, 11am-5pm Jan & Feb; Ⓤ Messberg)

Speicherstadt & HafenCity Sights

The Speicherstadt & HafenCity Story

The seven-storey red-brick warehouses lining the **Speicherstadt** archipelago stretch all the way to Baumwall in the world's largest continuous warehouse complex. Their neo-Gothic gables and (mostly) green copper roofs are reflected in the narrow canals of this free-port zone. Historic boats line the waterways.

A separate free port became necessary when Hamburg joined the German Customs Federation on signing up to the German Reich in 1871. An older neighbourhood was demolished – and 24,000 people displaced – to make room for the construction of the Speicherstadt from 1885 to 1927. This area was spared wartime destruction; in 2015 it made Unesco's World Heritage list in recognition of its historic role in rapidly expanding world trade.

The Speicherstadt merges into Europe's biggest inner-city urban development, **HafenCity**. Here, a long-derelict port area of 155 hectares is being redeveloped with restaurants, shops, apartments, schools and offices. In the next 20 years, it's anticipated that some 40,000 people will work and 12,000 will live here. For the moment, however, it can seem a bit bleak, as only some projects are complete and large swathes of land are vacant.

Hamburg Dungeon (p95)

Spicy's Gewürzmuseum
MUSEUM

 MAP P94, B2

This spice and herb museum invites you to exercise your olfaction to the fullest. (📞040-367 989; www.spicys.de; Am Sandtorkai 34; adult/child €5/2; ⊙10am-5pm; Ⓤ Messberg)

HafenCity Riverbus
BOATING

3 ◉ MAP P94, C2

Now here's something a little different – a 70-minute tour of the city in an amphibious bus, with 40 minutes spent on land and 30 minutes on the Elbe River. Commentary is in German only. (📞040-7675 7500; www.hafencityriverbus. de; Brooktorkai 16, Block 5; adult/child €29.50/20.50; ⊙every 90min from 10am Feb-Dec, last departures vary; Ⓤ Messberg)

Eating

For our money, the culinary offering in Speicherstadt and HafenCity is lagging a little behind the rest of the development. There are plenty of places to eat, but there are few that stand out. We expect that to change over the coming years.

Speicherstadt has a couple of excellent traditional restaurants amid its old restored warehouses. HafenCity has a few newish eateries but until it gets more built up, they have a slightly soulless feel among the never-ending construction.

Carls Brasserie
BISTRO €€

 4 MAP P94, A3

Facing the Elbphilharmonie, this casual place offers predominantly French cuisine, such as *croque-monsieur* and other toasts in the bistro, with a little more sophistication in the brasserie. The bistro offers better value. (☑040-300 322 400; www.carls-brasserie.de; Am Kaiserkai 69; bistro mains €9-13, brasserie mains €15-34; ⊙noon-11pm; ⓤBaumwall)

Strauchs Falco
INTERNATIONAL €€

 5 MAP P94, D2

The menu here is astonishingly broad (tapas, pizza, pasta, seafood) without compromising on quality. Their speciality is flame-grilled meats. (☑040-226 161 511; www.falco-hamburg.de; Koreastrasse 2; mains €10-28; ⊙noon-3pm & 5.30pm-midnight Mon-Fri, 12.30pm-midnight Sat & Sun; ⓤMessberg, Überseequartier)

Baakenpark

Opened in May 2018, **Baakenpark** (Map p94, F4; www.hafencity.com; Baakenallee; ⓤHafenCity Universität), on the southeastern reaches of HafenCity, is proof that the HafenCity development hasn't forgotten the need for parks. With kids' playgrounds, weekend concerts and even the occasional open-air cinema, it's a lovely place to escape the rigours of city life.

Fleetschlösschen
BISTRO €€

 6 MAP P94, C2

Timelessly cute, this former customs post overlooks a Speicherstadt canal and has a narrow steel spiral staircase to the toilets. There's barely room for 20 inside, but its outdoor seating areas are brilliant in sunny weather. Choose

Worth a Trip: Auswanderermuseum BallinStadt

Sort of a bookend for New York's Ellis Island, Hamburg's excellent emigration **museum** (☑040-3197 9160; www.ballinstadt.de; Veddeler Bogen 2; adult/child €13/7; ⊙10am-6pm Apr-Oct, to 4.30pm Nov-Mar; ⓡVeddel) looks at the conditions that drove about five million people to leave Germany for the US and South America in search of better lives from 1850 until the 1930s. Multilingual displays address the hardships endured before and during the voyage and upon arrival in the New World. About 4km southeast of the city centre, BallinStadt is easily reached by S-Bahn.

from sandwiches, soups, salads and various small plates; fish is a recurring them, as you'd expect from a place overseen by Daniel Wischer (p51). (📞040-3039 3210; www.fleetschloesschen.de; Brooktorkai 17; mains €10-20; ⏰8am-10pm; ⓈMessberg)

Bootshaus Grill & Bar

STEAK €€€

7 ❌ MAP P94, B3

Steaks in all their glory dominate proceedings here. We prefer them without sauces, but put us by the Elbe overlooking the water with a medium-rare rib-eye on our plate and we don't really care how they serve it. (📞040-3347 3744; www.

bootshaus-hafencity.de; Am Kaiserkai 19; lunch specials €11, mains €26-39; ⏰noon-3pm & 6-10pm Tue-Sat; Ⓤ Überseequartier)

Drinking

Nightlife in any meaningful form has yet to arrive in Speicherstadt and HafenCity. A few bars lie scattered around, and most restaurants stay open late and have outdoor tables in summer – Bootshaus Grill & Bar is one of the better choices. But this is not a neighbourhood you'd consider for after-dark action. Unlike most things around here, that's unlikely to change in the foreseeable future.

Fleetschlösschen (p97)

Worth a Trip: Tierpark Hagenbeck

The 2500 animals that live in Hamburg's **zoo** (☏040-530 0330; www.hagenbeck-tierpark.de; Lokstedter Grenzstrasse 2; adult/child from €20/15, combined ticket with aquarium €30/21; ⏱9am-7pm Jul & Aug, to 6pm Sep-Oct & Mar-Jun, to 4.30pm Nov-Feb, aquarium 9am-7pm Jul & Aug, to 6pm Sep-Jun; ⛎; ⒰Hagenbecks Tierpark) have open enclosures over 27 hectares. In addition to elephants, tigers, orangutans, toucans and other creatures, you'll find a replica Nepalese temple, a Japanese garden, an art deco gate and a huge aquarium. A petting zoo, pony rides, a miniature railway and playground mean you'll have to drag the kids away at the end of the day. It is 5km northwest of the centre.

Entertainment

Elbphilharmonie   CLASSICAL MUSIC

8 ☆ MAP P94, A3

Attending a concert here is an essential part of visiting Hamburg's most exciting architectural icon. With a full program, a number of different performance spaces and world-leading acoustics, it's a terrific experience, whatever you see. Advance bookings are always recommended. (☏040-3576 6666; www.elbphilharmonie.de; Platz der Deutschen Einheit 4; tickets €10-75; ⏱box office 11am-8pm; ⒰Baumwall)

Shopping

You'll find shops here and there in Speicherstadt and HafenCity, but it's still a work-in-progress without anything yet that catches the eye. The one exception, and it's an important one, are the shops attached to each museum – they range from cool to kitsch with the models at Miniatur Wunderland (p90), and the gift shop in the Elbphilharmonie (p86) the pick.

Explore

St Pauli & Reeperbahn

St Pauli has soul. The energy, creativity and, yes, even the vices of this perennial enfant terrible transform Hamburg daily into one of Europe's coolest cities. On a wet weekday morning, St Pauli appears a little worse for wear but when a party takes over Spielbundenplatz, there are few finer places to be.

St Pauli is rarely at its best in the morning. The only exception is Sunday mornings, when it's worth getting up early (or staying up late...) for the Fischmarkt (p102). Otherwise, a stroll along 930m-long Reeperbahn – always the starting point for exploring St Pauli – is a good way to get your bearings. If there's live music or anything else happening in Spielbudenplatz (p110), head there late afternoon. St Pauli in general, and Reeperbahn in particular, begin with a roar in the early evening and continue to crescendo in a tsunami of noise and light and music and all things risqué. All. Night.

Getting There & Around

S & **U** Reeperbahn S-Bahn station (lines S1, S2 and S3) and St Pauli U-Bahn station (U3) lie at either end of Reeperbahn. You'll have to walk from either to get to the Fischmarkt, but the main port area is right next to Landungsbrücken station (S1, S2, S3 and U3). In the north, Feldstrasse (U3) is the most useful station.

St Pauli & Reeperbahn Map on p106

Spielbudenplatz (p110) BILDAGENTUR-ONLINE/JOKO/ALAMY ©

Top Sights 📸
Fischmarkt

While other cities sleep off their Saturday-night hangover, Hamburg just never wants it all to end. And let's face it, few places on earth do Saturday nights like St Pauli... and continue on into the next day. This Sunday morning market is simply fabulous, a time when the entire city comes out to play. It's not yet 5am when the first customers begin to trundle in.

◉ **MAP P106, A8**

Grosse Elbstrasse 9

🕐 5am-9.30am Sun Apr-Oct, from 7am Nov-Mar

🚌 112 to Fischmarkt,
Ⓢ Reeperbahn

A Market in Full Swing

Every Sunday in the wee hours, some 70,000 locals and visitors descend upon the famous Fischmarkt in St Pauli, which has been running since 1703. Vendors artfully arrange their bananas, cherries, kumquats and whatever else they've picked up that week (some comes direct from farms but a lot comes from wholesalers). Others pile up eels, shellfish, cacti and all manner of goods.

Live Music

Live bands crank out cover versions of ancient German pop songs in the adjoining Fischauktionshalle (Fish Auction Hall). This is not the morning (and St Pauli is most definitely not the place) for playing around with the neighbourhood's favourite musical genre. You'll be singing along to the choruses in no time, especially if you've been up all night...

Street Theatre

The market also revels in its street theatre, with set-piece vaudeville acts that are a fun feature of proceedings. Its undisputed stars are the boisterous *Marktschreier* (market criers) who hawk their wares at full volume. 'Don't be shy, little girl,' a vendor might shout with a lascivious wink to a 60-year-old, waggling a piece of eel in front of her face. Almost always, the 'girl' blushes before taking a hearty bite as the crowd cheers.

Fish Sandwiches for Breakfast

There are numerous places selling *Fischbrötchen* (fish sandwiches) around the market. Normally a lunch or afternoon snack, pickled herrings and onions in a roll at six in the morning can suddenly seem strangely appealing. It's the perfect hangover cure.

★ Top Tips

o We can't tell you why, but the Fischmarkt just *seems* more enjoyable if you've been up all night in St Pauli, rather than rising early to join the crowds.

o Get here as early as you can to watch the sun rise over the harbour.

✕ Take a Break

Just up the hill and spilling out onto a quiet St Pauli square, Cafe Geyer (p116) is a lovely spot for a post-Fischmarkt coffee.

Hang around long enough after the market dies down and you can order lunch at Fischerhaus (p113), one of the better fish restaurants in the area.

Walking Tour 🚶

The Essence of St Pauli

Few neighbourhoods in Europe swagger quite like St Pauli. But for all its brashness and bright lights, St Pauli has an identity that defines it – one of solidarity, of openness to all, and of its ability to provide something for everyone. All across the neighbourhood, quintessentially St Pauli haunts, diverse as they are, capture that spirit.

Walk Facts

Start Café Mimosa;
Ⓤ St Pauli

End Lunacy; Ⓤ St Pauli

Length 2km

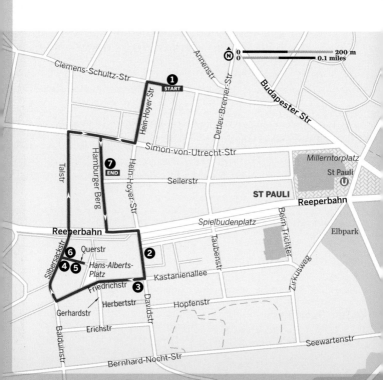

❶ Café Mimosa

This gem of a neighbourhood **cafe** (☎040-3202 7989; www.cafemimosa. de; Clemens-Schultz-Strasse 87; mains €4-12; ⏰10am-7pm Tue-Sun) is the go-to place for warm brioches, some of the yummiest cakes in town, plus daily changing lunch specials. Relax inside among theatrical flourishes or grab a table outside. It's a great place to plan your exploration of the surrounding streets.

❷ Davidwache

South of the Reeperbahn stands the star of many a German crime film and TV show, the **Davidwache** (Spielbudenplatz 31, cnr Davidstrasse). This brick police station, festooned with ornate ceramic tiles, is the base for 150 officers, who keep the lurid surrounds reasonably tame.

❸ Sankt Pauli Museum

To make historical sense of St Pauli, this **museum** (☎040-439 2080; www.sankt-pauli-museum. de; Davidstrasse 17; adult/concession €5/4; ⏰11am-6pm Mon-Wed, to 9pm Thu, to 11pm Fri, 10am-11pm Sat, 10am-6pm Sun) is an excellent place to start. It takes you back to the earliest days of the neighbourhood, brings to life many of its characters, and doesn't flinch from the seedy and the sinful.

❹ Zum Silbersack

A real St Pauli icon, **Zum Silbersack** (☎040-314 589; www.facebook. com/zumsilbersack1949; Silbersack-

strasse 9; ⏰5pm-1am Sun, to 3am Mon-Wed, to 4am Thu, 3pm-5am Fri & Sat) is one of our favourite pubs in the area. You'll find students, junkies, executives, greenies, millionaires and prostitutes there. Anything seems possible and it can be a little rough around the edges, but it's very St Pauli.

❺ Kiez Curry

All manner of *Currywurst* (there's even a vegan version) have made **Kiez Curry** (☎040-6367 3829; www. kiezcurry.de; Querstrasse 2; mains from €3; ⏰5pm-midnight Tue-Thu, to 5am Fri & Sat) an icon of St Pauli's nights. A currywurst at 4am after a hard night of partying just feels right in Hamburg...If you're really hungry, add the potato salad to your order.

❻ Kleine Haie Grosse Fische

St Pauli's version of the late-night kebab stop is this timeless **place** (☎0176-1033 7847; www.kleinehaie -grossefische.de; Querstrasse 4; mains from €4; ⏰6pm-midnight Wed & Thu, 2pm-4am Fri & Sat; Ⓢ Reeperbahn) serving fish sandwiches, as well as smoked fish and meats.

❼ Lunacy

This is a **bar** (☎040-3179 2726; www. lunacy-hh.de; Hamburger Berg 25; ⏰9pm-4am Sun-Thu, to dawn Fri & Sat) with attitude in the finest St Pauli tradition – the music stays pretty intense with punk, ska, rock and metal, and even the table football is played seriously in these parts.

St Pauli & Reeperbahn

KAROLINENVIERTEL

SCHANZENVIERTEL

HEILIGENGEISTFELD

Marktstr

Glashüttenstr

Feldstr

Marktstr

Sternstr

Beckstr

Schulterblatt

Neuer Pferdemarkt

Stresemannstr

Neuer Kamp

Neuer Pferdemarkt

Thadenstr

Gilbertstr

Bernstorffstr

Budapester Str

Annenstr

Hein-Hoyer-Str

Clemens-Schultz-Str

Grosse Freiheit

Paul-Roosen-Str

Otzenstr

Wohlers Allee

Holstenstr

Glacischaussee

Planten un Blomen

Grosse Wallanlagen

Flakturm IV

Beatles Tour

Feldstrasse

39 5

11

53

49

21

25 18

22 27 19

47

43

52

For reviews see

◉ Top Sights   p102
◎ Sights   p108
⊗ Eating   p111
⊗ Drinking   p114
⊕ Entertainment   p118
⊞ Shopping   p121

200 m
0.1 miles

A B C D

1 2 3 4

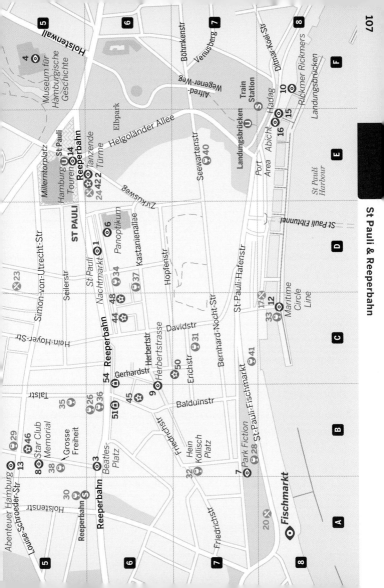

St Pauli & Reeperbahn

Sights

Even those not interested in lurid late nights usually pay a quick trip to St Pauli's Reeperbahn to see what the fuss is all about. Sure, it's tamer than the Amsterdam scene (which is itself becoming tamer), but it's still Europe's biggest in terms of the number of businesses. Long established as a party place, the Reeperbahn is flooded by crowds of thousands from around 4pm on weekends, cruising the lurid collection of bars, sex clubs, variety acts, pubs and cafes collectively known as the 'Kiez'. There are also museums and architectural showpieces to catch the eye.

St Pauli Nachtmarkt   MARKET

1 ⊚ MAP P106, D6

Wednesday late afternoon and evening is a terrific time to be in St Pauli when the weekly night market takes over Spielbudenplatz with food stalls, live bands (usually around 6pm or 7pm) and plenty of comfy chairs to knock back a beer. (Spielbudenplatz; ⊘4-11pm Wed Apr-Sep, to 10pm Oct-Mar)

Tanzende Türme   ARCHITECTURE

2 ⊚ MAP P106, E6

Watching over the eastern gateway to St Pauli since 2011, the 'Dancing Towers' are a Hamburg icon. The two towers buck and weave by up to 3m from the vertical, making it appear like a couple dancing; a legendary dancehall once stood on the site and it's a fitting introduction to this neighbourhood that loves to party. It's wonderfully lit at night. (Reeperbahn 1; ⓤSt Pauli)

Beatles-Platz   SQUARE

3 ⊚ MAP P106, B6

Designed like a vinyl record, Beatles-Platz has abstract steel sculptures resembling cookie cutters of the Fab Four (including a hybrid of Ringo Starr and Pete Best). (Ⓢ Reeperbahn)

Museum für Hamburgische Geschichte   MUSEUM

4 ⊚ MAP P106, F5

Hamburg's history museum has lots of kid-friendly features: it's chock-full of intricate ship models, has a large model train set, and is home to the actual bridge of the steamship *Werner*. As it chronicles the city's evolution, it reveals titbits such as the fact that the Reeperbahn was once the home of rope makers (*Reep* means 'rope'). There is a good exhibit on the history of the city's Jewish population. (Museum of Hamburg History; ☏040-428 412 380; www.hamburg museum.de; Holstenwall 24; adult/child €9.50/free; ⊘10am-5pm Mon & Wed-Sat, to 6pm Sun; 🚻; ⓤSt Pauli)

Flakturm IV   ARCHITECTURE

5 ⊚ MAP P106, E2

Rising up from the northern reaches of St Pauli, this brooding concrete structure was built during WWII as an anti-aircraft defence position but doubled as a bunker or shelter for those fleeing bombardment – a rather strange combination when you think about it. Around 18,000 people could shelter here behind the 3.5m-thick walls. Now it's a nightclub, Uebel und Gefährlich (p117). (Feldstrasse 66; [U]Feldstrasse)

Panoptikum

MUSEUM

6 MAP P106, D6

If wax museums are your thing, this a decent version with more than 120 figures spread over four floors. Everyone gets a run, from Queen Elizabeth and Pope Benedict XVI to Angelina Jolie and St Pauli identity Olivia Jones. (☏040-310 317; www.panoptikum.de; Spielbudenplatz 3; adult/child €6.50/4.50; ⏰11am-9pm Mon-Fri, to midnight Sat, from 10am Sun; [U]St Pauli)

Park Fiction

PARK

7 MAP P106, B7

Hamburg's maritime tableau spreads out before this park created by local residents and overlooking the Elbe. Pick up some beer and have your own sunset happy hour while lounging on the grass under the fake palm trees. (www.park-fiction.net; Antonistrasse; [S]Reeperbahn)

Star Club Memorial

MEMORIAL

8 MAP P106, B5

The seminal venue for the Beatles opened in 1962. It has since burnt down and there is a sad historical marker. Thai karaoke now echoes off the walls. (Grosse Freiheit 39; [S]Reeperbahn)

St Pauli & Reeperbahn Sights

Beatles-Platz

MC PHOTO/OHDE/ALAMY ©

Spielbudenplatz

There always seems to be something going on in Spielbudenplatz. Wednesdays is the St Pauli Nachtmarkt (p108), but other semiregular occurrences include:

○ Live music and container bars nightly from 4pm from April to September.

○ Street-food trucks turn up on Thursdays from 5pm to 11pm from April to October, and 6pm to 9pm from January to March.

○ Twice a year, a flea market takes over the *platz*, usually on the first Sunday in June and September.

○ Also twice a year, in May and September, the St Pauli Food Truck Festival (p120) arrives.

○ St Pauli's Christmas Market (from late November to 23 December) is a typically irreverent affair.

For more information, visit www.spielbudenplatz.eu.

Herbertstrasse STREET

9 ◎ MAP P106, B6

Along Davidstrasse, a painted tin wall bars views into Herbertstrasse, a block-long bordello that's off-limits to men under 18 and to women of all ages. It's the notorious sinful centre of the district. (Herbertstrasse; S Reeperbahn)

Rickmer Rickmers MUSEUM

10 ◎ MAP P106, F8

The 1886 three-masted steel windjammer *Rickmer Rickmers* is now a museum ship; from the restaurant on deck you have fine harbour views. (☏040-319 5959; www.rickmer-rickmers.de; Ponton 1a; adult/child €5/3; ◷10am-6pm; S Landungsbrücken)

Beatles Tour WALKING

11 ◎ MAP P106, E2

For an entertaining look at the Beatles in Hamburg, try this Beatles tour offered by the fun and engaging Stephanie Hempel. It starts from the U-Bahn station Feldstrasse and includes museum entry and a small concert. (☏040-3003 3790; www.hempels-musictour.com; tour €28; ◷6pm Sat Apr-Nov; U Feldstrasse)

Maritime Circle Line BOATING

12 ◎ MAP P106, C8

Harbour shuttle service connecting Hamburg's maritime cultural attractions, including the Auswanderermuseum BallinStadt and Miniatur Wunderland. The entire loop takes around 95 minutes; you can hop on or off at any of its stops. (☎040-2849 3963; www.maritime-circle-line.de; Landungsbrücken 10, Jetty 10; adult/child €16/8; Ⓤ & ⓈLandungsbrücken)

Abenteuer Hamburg TOURS

13 ◎ MAP P106, B5

There are a number of tours on offer here, but the one that really gets under the skin of St Pauli is the adults-only 'Sex & Crime' tour (€23), which takes you through the sex and sleaze of St Pauli with plenty of humour and anecdotes along the way. (☎040-7566 3399; www.abenteuer-hamburg.com; Simon-von-Utrecht-Strasse 1; ⓈReeperbahn)

Hamburg Touren TOURS

14 ◎ MAP P106, E5

This dynamic company organises tours to the Elbphilharmonie, but it's like a decoy for their mischievous side, namely their 'St Pauli by Night' (€24.90) and 'Sex, Drugs & Currywurst' (€29.90) tours of St Pauli after dark. Both of the latter tours last two hours and leave at 8pm from the entrance to the St Pauli U-Bahn station. Advance bookings recommended. (☎040-3863 3997; www.hamurg-erlebniswelt.de; tours €15-30; ⓊSt Pauli)

Hadag BOATING

15 ◎ MAP P106, E8

Harbour tours plus more adventuresome trips to the Lower Elbe (April to September). Also offers a hop-on, hop-off service along the Elbe. (☎040-311 7070; www.hadag.de; Brücke 2; 1hr harbour tour adult/child from €18/9; ⊙daily Apr-Sep, Sat & Sun Oct-Mar; Ⓤ & ⓈLandungsbrücken)

Abicht BOATING

16 ◎ MAP P106, E8

This company's harbour tours are rightly popular; it also offers Saturday-evening tours taking you past the illuminated warehouses (departure times vary according to tides). (☎040-317 8220; www.abicht.de; Brücke 1; 1hr tour adult/child €20/10; ⊙noon Apr-Oct; ⓊLandungsbrücken, ⓈLandungsbrücken)

Eating

Note that it's easy to escape the clamour of St Pauli's manufactured sleaze by getting just a few streets off the Reeperbahn, especially to the north where you can find quiet squares and cool cafes. In fact, the further you get from the Reeperbahn, the better your odds of having something tasty to eat (unless it's 4am, in which case the gaggle of fast-food spots along this notorious street will do just fine).

Right on the water you'll find a plethora of ice-cream stands, fried-fish stalls and other victuals-pushers for the strolling masses.

Fischbrötchenbude Brücke 10 SEAFOOD €

17 ⊗ MAP P106, C8

There are a gazillion fish sandwich vendors in Hamburg, but we're going to stick our neck out and say that this vibrant, clean and contemporary outpost makes the best. Try a classic *Bismarck* (pickled herring) or *Matjes* (brined herring), or treat yourself to a bulging shrimp sandwich. Lovely tables outside. (☑040-3339 9339; www.bruecke-10.de; Landungsbrücken, Pier 10; sandwiches €3-9.50; ☻10am-10pm; S & ⓤLandungsbrücken)

Pauline

CAFE €

18 ☒ MAP P106, C2

Tucked away on a residential street and as good for breakfast as for lunch, this classy cafe is enduringly popular with locals, but they can't keep it all to themselves. The small but thoughtfully chosen lunch menu includes quiche, salad or pasta, while the break-

fasts are excellent. The Sunday brunch (with sittings at 10am and 12.30pm) is excellent. (☑040-4135 9964; www.pauline-hamburg.de; Neuer Pferdemarkt 3; mains €3-10, Sun brunch €18.70; ☻8.30am-4pm Mon-Fri, 9am-6pm Sat, 10am-6pm Sun; ⓤFeldstrasse)

Konditorei Holger Rönnfeld

BAKERY €

19 ☒ MAP P106, C4

Sweet offerings abound at this aromatic and traditional bakery. Try a *nussecken*, a crunchy, nutty, triangular-shaped pastry. (☑040-313 536; www.hochzeitstorten-hamburg.de; Hein-Hoyer-Strasse 52; snacks from €2; ☻6.30am-6pm Mon-Fri, to 4pm Sat; SReeperbahn, ⓤSt Pauli)

Fish roll at Fischbrötchenbude Brücke 10 (p111)

DIRK RENCKHOFF/ALAMY ©

Fischerhaus
SEAFOOD €€

20 ⊗ MAP P106, A8

Arguably the pick of the sit-down fish restaurants down in the Fischmarkt, Fischerhaus has three different dining spaces – the views are better from the Hafenblick room, but it's more casual and kid-friendly at Rustikal, where prices also tend to be slightly lower. Fried fish is a speciality, but you could pick anything here and leave satisfied. (☏040-314 053; www.restaurant-fischerhaus.de; St Pauli Fischmarkt 14; mains €9-25; ☺11.30am-10.30pm; ⓤReeperbahn)

Markt Koenig
GERMAN €€

21 ⊗ MAP P106, D2

Don't be fooled by the location, surrounded by a food hall and next to a supermarket. Markt Koenig is a bright modern place that does a range of local specialities, including various versions of schnitzel, a couple of roasts and curry bratwurst. They also serve breakfasts and well-priced steaks. (☏040-4309 6135; www.markt-koenig.de; Neuer Kamp 31, Rindermarkthalle; mains €9-18; ☺10am-midnight Sun-Thu, to 1am Fri & Sat; ⓤFeldstrasse)

Brachmanns Galeron
GERMAN €€

22 ⊗ MAP P106, C4

Schwabisch specialities (from the area around Stuttgart) dominate this light-filled restaurant and whisky bar – the combination of the two means you could easily spend a whole night here without ever needing to leave. Dishes include *Spätzle,* a pasta-like dish. (☏040-6730 5123; www.brachmanns-galeron.de; Hein-Hoyer-Strasse 60; mains €9-17; ⓤSt Pauli, Feldstrasse)

Le Kaschemme
EUROPEAN €€

23 ⊗ MAP P106, D5

The perfect place for a meal while you plan your night out in St Pauli, this clean-lined pub has a good menu of dishes that range from Italian to German. There are sidewalk tables and when you're ready to move on, you can't go far in this cafe-filled area until you find another good spot. (☏040-5190 6370; www.le-kaschemme.de; Rendsburger Strasse 14; mains €8-17; ☺6pm-midnight Mon-Sat; ⓤSt Pauli)

Clouds
INTERNATIONAL €€€

24 ⊗ MAP P106, E6

Arguably St Pauli's most prestigious table, Clouds, on the 23rd floor of the Tanzende Türme (p108), is an elegant space with marvellous views out over the city. The menu is dominated by steaks and a few French touches; you'll need to book ahead at all times and dress nicely. After your meal, head upstairs to Heaven's Nest (p114). (☏040 3099 3280; www.clouds-hamburg.de; Reeperbahn 1, Tanzende Türme; mains €29-54; ☺11.30am-2pm & 5-11pm Mon-Fri, 5-11pm Sat & Sun; ⓤSt Pauli)

Nil

INTERNATIONAL €€€

25 ✖ MAP P106, C2

There's a lot happening here at this hip tri-level restaurant. The varied and inspired slow-food menu is steered by the seasons and whatever regional suppliers have in store. Flavour pairings can be adventurous. The summer garden tables are dreamy. (☎040-439 7823; www.restaurant-nil. de; Neuer Pferdemarkt 5; mains €19-28; ⏱6-10.30pm Wed-Sun; Ⓤ Feldstrasse)

Drinking

St Pauli and Reeperbahn are the epicentres of Hamburg's legendary nightlife. There's so much going on here that you may well need a number of nights to truly experience even a representative sample. Neighbourhood bars and nightclubs jostle for street space with the strip clubs, sex shows and late-night tattoo parlours, and, in true St Pauli spirit, the full gamut of Hamburg society turns up here at some stage – most places will happily serve a beer to anyone with €3. You can still hear up-and-coming music acts.

Zur Ritze

BAR

26 Ⓟ MAP P106, B6

The uniqueness of this Reeperbahn classic begins from the moment you pass through the long laneway and between the legs of the large 'receptionist' painted over the door. Inside, it's a serious drinking den, that even draws a

few local celebrities. Down in the basement is a boxing gym. It's very eclectic in the finest St Pauli tradition. (www.zurritze.com; Reeperbahn 140; ⏱5pm-6am Mon-Thu, from 2pm Fri-Sun; Ⓢ Reeperbahn)

Café du Port

CAFE

27 Ⓟ MAP P106, C4

One of our favourite little perches in St Pauli, this gorgeous cafe does buttery croissants, cakes and other pastries, with fine coffee to nurse as you look for an excuse to linger in this intimate space. (☎040-6483 3238; www.cafe-du-port. de; Hein-Hoyer-Strasse 56; pastries from €3; ⏱9am-7pm Sun-Tue & Thu, to 8pm Fri & Sat; Ⓤ St Pauli, Ⓢ Reeperbahn)

Golden Pudel Club

BAR, LIVE MUSIC

28 Ⓟ MAP P106, B7

In a 19th-century bootleggers' jail, this tiny bar-club is run by members of the legendary ex-punk band Die Goldenen Zitronen and is an essential stop on the St Pauli party circuit. Night after night it gets packed to the rafters for its countercultural vibe, quality bands and DJs, and relaxed crowd. (☎040-3197 9930; www.pudel.com; St-Pauli-Fischmarkt 27; ⏱11pm-6am; Ⓢ Reeperbahn)

Clouds Bar

COCKTAIL BAR

This elegant bar, above Clouds Restaurant (24 ✖ MAP P106, E6) at the eastern entrance to St Pauli, is popular with an upmarket crowd

The Beatles in Hamburg

It was the summer of 1960 and a fledgling band from Liverpool had been assured a paying gig in Hamburg, if only it could come up with a drummer. After a frantic search, Pete Best joined John Lennon, Paul McCartney, George Harrison and Stuart Sutcliffe in August that year.

The Beatles opened on the notorious **Grosse Freiheit** to seedy crowds of drunks. After 48 consecutive nights of six-hour sessions, the Beatles' innate musical genius had been honed. The magnetism of the group that would rock the world began drawing loyal crowds. But complications ensued when an underage George was deported in November, and Paul and Pete were arrested for attempted arson. All escaped the German authorities and returned to England. There, as 'The Beatles: Direct from Hamburg', they had their Merseyside breakthrough.

In 1961 the Beatles returned to Hamburg. During a 92-night stint, they made their first professional recording. Soon manager extraordinaire Brian Epstein and the recording genius George Martin arrived on the scene. The Beatles began their career with EMI; Pete Best was replaced by Ringo Starr, a more professional drummer; Stuart Sutcliffe quit the band; and they went on to fame and fortune.

who come here for the highballs (of course!) and perfectly mixed cocktails. When the weather is fine and clear, head to the lounge chairs at the open-air Heaven's Nest right on the summit. The dress code is 'casual elegant'. (Heaven's Nest; 📞040-3099 3280; www.clouds-hamburg.de/bar; Reeperbahn 1, Tanzende Türme; ⏰11.30am-late Mon-Fri, from noon Sat & Sun; Ⓤ St Pauli)

Indra Club   CLUB

29 📍 MAP P106, B5

The Beatles' small first venue is open again and has live acts some nights. The interior is vastly different from the 1960s and there is a

fine beer garden. (www.indramusik club.com; 64 Grosse Freiheit; ⏰9pm-late Wed-Sun; Ⓢ Reeperbahn)

Molotow   CLUB

30 📍 MAP P106, A5

This legendary indie club still rocks on as hot 'n heavy as ever after moving to new digs when its old location was torn down. (📞040-310 845; www.molotowclub.com; Nobistor 14; ⏰6pm-late; Ⓢ Reeperbahn)

Komet Musik Bar   BAR

31 📍 MAP P106, C7

Vinyl and only vinyl spins at this treasure of a music bar. Nightly themes range from ska and rocksteady to '60s garage punk and hip hop. Order a Helga, a sweetish house drink that will have everything sounding dreamy in no time. (📞040-2786 8686; www.komet-st-pauli.de; Erichstrasse 11; ⏰9pm-late; 🚇St Pauli)

Cafe Geyer CAFE

32 🍴 MAP P106, B7

You could come here for the breakfast, or the reasonable meals. But we love it in spring when the sun is shining and the view of the blossom trees from the outdoor tables makes this a quietly beautiful perch to nurse a wine or coffee. (📞040-2393 6122; Hein-Köllisch-Platz 4; ⏰10am-1am; 🚉Reeperbahn)

Frau Hedis Tanzkaffee CLUB

33 🍴 MAP P106, C8

On a boat moored permanently at pier 10, this unusual nightclub is also the ultimate party boat. A full program of visiting DJs keeps things interesting, and if you get the munchies, Hamburg's best fisch-brötchen (p111) is nearby. (📞0176 8306 1071; www.frauhedi.de; Landungs-brücken Brücke 10; €6-15; ⏰7pm-late Wed-Sat; 🚉 & 🚇Landungsbrücken)

Docks CLUB

34 🍴 MAP P106, D6

They keep it fairly simple and none-too-challenging at this long-standing Reeperbahn club – house in all its forms, reggae, downtempo and hip-hop dominate and they'll rarely stray far from these pa-

Docks

rameters. That's why it has a loyal following. (☏040-3178 830; www.docks-prinzenbar.de; Spielbudenplatz 19; ⏱11pm-6am Fri & Sat; Ⓤ St Pauli)

Wunderbar
GAY

35 🚇 MAP P106, B5

An extravagant gay bar with luminous red interiors, Wunderbar has been around since the 1990s and shows no signs of slowing down. Up-for-a-good-time DJs spin everything from Schlager to House. (☏040-317 4444; www.wunderbar-hamburg.de; Talstrasse 14; ⏱10pm-late; Ⓢ Reeperbahn)

Moondoo
CLUB

36 🚇 MAP P106, B6

Amidst all the sex shows and sleaze, Reeperbahn does good, old-fashioned nightclubs rather well – Moondoo is a fun, casual place with terrific DJs (resident and touring). (☏040-3197 5530; www.moondoo.de; Reeperbahn 136; ⏱11pm-7am Thu-Sat; Ⓢ Reeperbahn)

Prinzenbar
BAR, CLUB

37 🚇 MAP P106, D6

With its cheeky cherubs, stucco flourishes and sparkling chandeliers, this intimate club has luxe looks but is in fact a former cinema that now hosts stylish electro parties, concerts, queer bashes and indie nights in the heart of St Pauli. (☏040-3178 8310; www.docks-prinzen bar.de; Kastanienallee 20; ⏱10pm-4am or later; Ⓢ Reeperbahn, Ⓤ St Pauli)

Gretel & Alfons
BAR

38 🚇 MAP P106, B5

A late-night cafe and bar that is little changed from when the Beatles would unwind here after shows. (www.gretelundalfons.de; Grosse Freiheit 29; ⏱6pm-6am; Ⓢ Reeperbahn)

Uebel und Gefährlich
CLUB

39 🚇 MAP P106, E2

DJ sets, live music and parties rock this soundproof WWII bunker. Doors open around 7pm weekdays but as late as midnight on Friday and Saturday. (☏040-3179 3610; www.uebelundgefaehrlich.com; Feldstrasse 66; Ⓤ Feldstrasse)

Tower Bar
LOUNGE

40 🚇 MAP P106, E7

For a low-key evening with harbour views that will keep you entranced, drop by this 14th-floor lounge at the Hotel Hafen. (☏040-311 13; www.hotel-hafen-hamburg.de; Seewartenstrasse 9; ⏱6pm-2am; Ⓢ & Ⓤ Landungsbrücken)

StrandPauli
BAR

41 🚇 MAP P106, C7

Tuesday is tango night at StrandPauli, a *Gilligan's Island* stretch of sand built over the water overlooking the busy docks. (☏040-2261 3105; www.strandpauli.de; St-Pauli-Hafenstrasse 89; ⏱11am-11pm; 🚌112)

Entertainment

In a neighbourhood that loves an audience, it should scarcely surprise that entertainment options abound. Storied live music venues are an essential element in St Pauli's after-dark fame, but there are also theatres, a near-mythical football stadium, and shows that blur the line between striptease and burlesque.

Mojo Club
JAZZ

42 ⭐ MAP P106, E6

This legendary Hamburg jazz club inhabits the fab basement of the Tanzende Türme (p108) office towers. Stellar local and international acts take to the stage here and it's always worth checking what's on. Great atmosphere, great acoustics, knowledgeable jazz crowd – it's one of Hamburg's best nights out. Opening hours vary, but most acts take to the stage around 8pm. (📞040-319 1999; www.mojo.de; Reeperbahn 1, Tanzende Türme; from €17; 🕖7pm-late; Ⓤ St Pauli)

Gruenspan
LIVE MUSIC

43 ⭐ MAP P106, B4

Around since the 1960s, Gruenspan has evolved since its time as a notorious drug den into one of St Pauli's best live music venues. Just about any musical genre can take to the stage here, but they seem to have a particular fondness for singer-songwriters – check the website to see if what's on suits your mood. (📞040-313 616; www.gruenspan.de; Grosse Freiheit 58; 🕕6pm-late; Ⓢ Reeperbahn)

St Pauli Theater
THEATRE

44 ⭐ MAP P106, C6

A dynamic program of high-quality, sometimes-offbeat theatre is the hallmark here. If you speak German, it can be a great night out. (📞040-4711 0666; www.st-pauli-theater.de; Spielbudenplatz 29-30; Ⓢ Reeperbahn, Ⓤ St Pauli)

Hasenschaukel
LIVE MUSIC

45 ⭐ MAP P106, B6

The booking policy at this unhurried pocket-size club with plush

On the Wane?

While the sex industry is still in full swing, some of the harsher edges are gone, although prostitutes dressed as schoolgirls are still in evidence. The once 'daring' sex shops are now marked by tired displays of sun-faded dildos in the windows. Herbertstrasse is still around, with prostitutes sitting behind glass as they famously do in Amsterdam. With so much still on show, many can't resist some safe titillation and on summer evenings tour groups of bug-eyed tourists jostle each other along the streets.

Strandpauli (p117)

decor skews towards lo-fi indie-folk-rock and usually features prestardom international artists along with DJ sets. Grab a vegan midnight snack if the vintage doll lamps get too trippy after a few beers. (☏040-1801 2721; www.hasenschaukel.de; Silbersackstrasse 17; ⏰9pm-1am Tue-Thu & Sun, to 4am Fri & Sat; Ⓢ Reeperbahn)

Kaiserkeller   LIVE MUSIC

46 ⭐ MAP P106, B5

One of the more respectable clubs today on the Grosse Freiheit, this second venue for the Beatles survives in a much-altered form with regular live acts. (Grosse Freiheit 36; Ⓢ Reeperbahn)

Millerntor-Stadion   STADIUM

47 ⭐ MAP P106, D3

Favourite local football team FC St Pauli plays at home in the multi-use Millerntor stadium. (☏040-3178 7451; www.fcstpauli.com; Heiligengeistfeld; Ⓤ Feldstrasse)

Schmidt Tivoli   THEATRE

48 ⭐ MAP P106, C6

This plush theatre stages a cornucopia of saucy musical reviews, comedies, soap operas and variety shows. Midnight shows follow the main performance. The newly opened adjoining **Schmidtchen** showcases young talent in a smaller venue. (☏040-3177 8899; www.tivoli.de; Spielbudenplatz 27-28; Ⓤ St Pauli)

Best St Pauli Festivals

Schlagermove

St Pauli is taken over in mid-July by **Schlagermove** (www.schlager move.de), a typically extravagant street parade. Everyone dresses up in a rather fun 1970s fashion to celebrate German-language disco pop songs. It takes place across the neighbourhood from the port area to the Reeperbahn. As you can imagine, the party spills over into the bars and nightclubs...

Reeperbahn Festival

This happening live-music **celebration** (www.reeperbahnfestival.com) in September covers every musical genre imaginable and fills St Pauli's venues (from seedy nightclubs to churches!) with crowds and quality performances. In 2018 some events were even held in the newly minted Elbphilharmonie (p86). Download the festival app to help make sense of it all.

St Pauli Food Truck Festival

Two times a year (usually mid-May and early September), the street-food **trucks** (www.spielbudenplatz.eu; Spielbudenplatz) roll into St Pauli's Spielbudenplatz and stick around for four or five days.

Hamburger Kabarett-Festival

Based at St Pauli Theater (p118), this cabaret **festival** (www.st-pauli -theater.de; ⊙Apr; Ⓤ St Pauli) has been running for more than three decades. The nightly program lasts for nearly a month and sometimes spills over into May.

Knust   LIVE PERFORMANCE

49 ⭐ MAP P106, D2

In addition to excellent live music gigs and experimental DJ sets, this former slaughterhouse hosts a variety of acts from acoustic raves to spoken word. (📞040-8797 6230; www.knusthamburg.de; Neuer Kamp 30; 7pm-late; Ⓤ Feldstrasse)

Queen Calavera   LIVE PERFORMANCE

50 ⭐ MAP P106, C7

An essential part of the St Pauli night, this burlesque show in a tiny venue divides visitors. Some love it as a less sleazy option to the table-dancing venues, others decry the short performances. Make up your own mind. (📞040-8515 8795; www. home-of-burlesque.com; Gerhardstrasse 7; €10-15; ⊙10pm-2am Thu, to 4am Fri & Sat, shows 11pm; Ⓢ Reeperbahn)

Shopping

Shopping is not St Pauli's strong suit, although you'll find a few places to spend your money, especially beyond Reeperbahn.

In the areas of Schanzenviertel and Karolinenviertel, Hamburg's countercultural scene has retro and vintage clothing and music shops, particularly along Marktstrasse, where you'll find everything from '70s sportswear to Bollywood fashions. Bartelsstrasse is another good bet for unusual wares.

Crazy Jeans   CLOTHING

51 🔒 MAP P106, B6

Black is everything here, with leather studs and all manner of pirate motifs filling this St Pauli classic. A few brand names turn up from time to time, but it's mostly about taking a slightly angry, sideways glance at life. (📞040-7402 3757; Reeperbahn 127; 🕑noon-10pm; Ⓢ Reeperbahn)

Ars Japonica   ARTS & CRAFTS

52 🔒 MAP P106, C4

Exquisite Japanese works of miniature and other art, as well as some homewares in the same vein; pieces adorned with Japanese calligraphy are a recurring theme. It's only small, but everything here is in perfect taste. (📞040-319 3875; www.arsjaponica.de; Hein-Hoyer-Strasse 48; 🕑1-5pm Tue-Fri, 10.30am-2pm Sat; Ⓢ Reeperbahn, Ⓤ St Pauli)

Flohschanze   MARKET

53 🔒 MAP P106, E1

Hamburg's best flea market is nirvana for thrifty trinket hunters and vintage junkies, with hundreds of vendors holding forth outdoors in the hip Karolinenviertel. (Neuer Kamp 30; 🕑8am-4pm Sat; Ⓤ Feldstrasse)

Loonies   CLOTHING

54 🔒 MAP P106, C6

St Pauli logos emblazon the shirts, other clothing and accessories here, and there's plenty of other retro fashion choices to enhance your local street cred. We were very tempted by the vinyl Air Zaire or Pan Am carry-on bags. (📞040-317 4316; www.loonies.de; Reeperbahn 115; 🕑noon-9pm Sun-Thu, to 10pm Fri & Sat; Ⓢ Reeperbahn)

Explore ⬡
Altona & Elbmeile

One of the coolest corners of Hamburg, Altona is many visitors' favourite neighbourhood. Its village-like feel is endlessly appealing, a quiet world of stylish, sometimes quirky attractions that include terrific restaurants, drinking holes and shops. It's at its best west of the S-Bahn and train stations. Down the hill and down by the water, a string of restaurants stretch along the Elbmeile.

Morning is a good time to begin. You could pop into the museum (p128), but otherwise sights are thin on the ground. Instead you'll find yourself enjoying the bird-song and letting Altona's understated appeal take hold as you make your way from cafe to boutique and back again. Having immersed yourself in Altona's charms, head south towards the water. If you're lucky and it's a fine day, from Altonaer Balkon (p128) you'll love the views out over the Elbe, its silhouetted cranes and the endless movement of Hamburg's port. Descending the hill, Altona's waterfront is worth lingering over – the choices for cafes and bars and restaurants is ample.

Getting There & Around

[S] Altona's train station handles long-distance services; the S-Bahn station covers lines S1, S2 and S3 of the inner urban subway network, as well as S11 and S31. Other useful stations in the neighbourhood's northeast include Sternschanze (U3) and Feldstrasse (U3).

⛴ Ferries or bus 112 connect Elbmeile with St Pauli and the city centre.

Altona & Elbmeile Map on p126

Walking Tour 🥾

Ottensen:
Hamburg's Quiet Achiever

*Altona in general, and Ottensen in particular, is
where many visitors fall in love with Hamburg.
There are few attractions here, at least not in the
traditional sense. Instead, you'll feel like you've
stumbled into Hamburg as it goes about its daily
life. Neither showy nor extravagant, Ottensen,
west of the train station, could be Hamburg's
coolest corner.*

Walk Facts
Start Mikkels; Ⓢ Altona
End Aurel; Ⓢ Altona
Length 2km

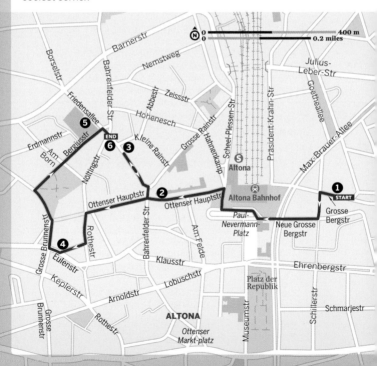

❶ Klippkroog

We lost track of the number of times a local told us this is their favourite **cafe** (☎040-5724 4368; www.klippkroog.de; Grosse Bergstrasse 255; mains €7-18; ⏰9am-midnight Mon-Sat, to 6pm Sun). Their classic dish of green asparagus, new potatoes and local ham is excellent, but there are plenty of lighter touches with an emphasis on local ingredients and recipes. The wooden tables, a light-filled space and great coffee round things out nicely.

❷ Søstrene Grene

The Altona outpost of this designer (yet affordable) Danish **homewares shop** (www.sostrene grene.com; Ottenser Hauptstrasse 20; ⏰10am-8pm Mon-Wed & Sat, to 9pm Thu & Fri) is a neighbourhood favourite and has an array of homewares that capture the essence of Scandinavian design – simple yet stylish, functional and often fun.

❸ Mikkels

Even if you miss the morning at this cheery **cafe** (☎040-7699 5072; www.mikkels.de; Kleine Rainstrasse 10; mains from €4.50; ⏰9am-6pm Mon-Sat, 10am-6pm Sun) which mixes affability with pastel style, you can still sit outside and catch the afternoon sun. Baked goods are fabulous and egg dishes are all-organic. The coffee? Good as you'd expect.

❹ Atelier Nigoh

Original prints and postcards, many of which are pop-art originals and signed by the artist, Nina Hasselluhn herself, are worth browsing through at this lovely small **studio** (☎040-6579 6995; www.nigoh.de; Eulenstrasse 62; ⏰11am-12.30pm & 1.30-7pm Tue-Fri, 11am-4pm Sat). We especially like the silhouette pieces of Hamburg port, which make a terrific souvenir of your visit, but there's so much to turn the head here. Nina also runs painting courses.

❺ GaumenGanoven

We *love* this **place** (☎0176-3293 5179; www.gaumenganoven.de; Friedensallee 7-9; mains from €5; ⏰noon-3pm & 6-10pm Tue & Wed, noon-3pm & 6-11pm Thu, to 1am Fri). A fun, brick-lined setting is the backdrop for little morsels – rather like tapas or antipasto (here they're called '*dinger*') – that you take, eat and then tally up when you're done. It works on the honour system, and boy does it work. Tastes often come in surprising combinations like prawns with mango-chilli and sesame, or octopus with hummus.

❻ Aurel

One of our favourite drinking holes in Altona, **Aurel** (☎040-390 2727; Bahrenfelder Strasse 157; ⏰10.30am-3am Mon-Thu, to 5am Fri & Sat, to 1am Sun) is warmly intimate by day, cool and classy by night – in the finest Hamburg tradition, it doesn't seem to matter what time it is. A DJ livens things up on weekend nights (mostly house). Our only complaint? It can get real smoky in there...

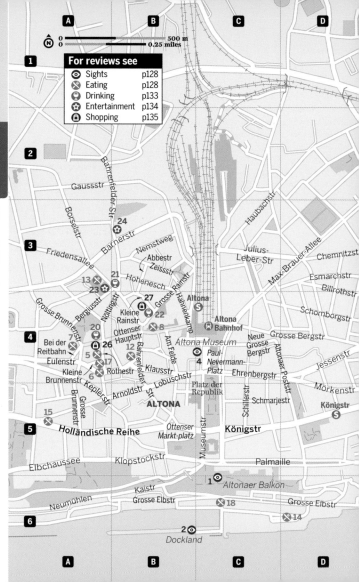

For reviews see

◉	Sights	p128
✕	Eating	p128
🍷	Drinking	p133
★	Entertainment	p134
🛍	Shopping	p135

0   500 m
0   0.25 miles

Gaussstr

Borselstr

Bahrenfelder Str

Barnerstr

Nemstweg

Friedensallee

Abbestr

Zeissstr

Hohenesch

24

Grosse Rainstr

Hahnenkamp

Julius-
Leber-Str

Chemnitzstr

Haubachstr

Max-Brauer-Allee

Esmarchstr

Billrothstr

Schomborgstr

13

23

21

Grosse Brunnenstr

Bergiusstr

Nöltingstr

27

Kleine
Rainstr

22

Altona
Ⓢ

**Altona
Bahnhof**
Ⓡ

Neue
Grosse
Bergstr

Grosse Bergstr

Altonaer Poststr

Jessenstr

20

7

26

Ottenser
Hauptstr

8

12

Am felde

Altona Museum

Paul-
Nevermann-
Platz

4

Ehrenbergstr

Mörkenstr

Bei der
Reitbahn

Eulenstr

5

17

Rothestr

Kleine
Brunnenstr

Keplerstr

Arnoldstr

Klausstr

Lobuschstr

ALTONA

Platz der
Republik

Schillerstr

Schmarjestr

Königstr
Ⓢ

6

Grosse
Brunnenstr

15

Holländische Reihe

Ottenser
Markt-platz

Museumstr

Königstr

Elbchaussee

Klopstockstr

Palmaille

Kaistr

Grosse Elbstr

1

Altonaer Balkon

18

Grosse Elbstr

14

Neumühlen

6

2

Dockland

E   F   G   H

Sternschanzenpark
Sternschanze

Langenfelder Str
Altonaer Str
Sternschanze

Bartelstr
Sternschanze

Max-Brauer-Allee
Lippmannstr
Susannenstr
10   ⊗ **11**   Lagerstr

Stresemannstr
19
9
3
Rote
Flora
SCHANZENVIERTEL

Kampstr   ⊗ **16**

Schulterblatt
Schanzenstr
Vorwerkstr

Wohlers Allee
Bernstorffstr
🔒 **25**
KAROLINENVIERTEL

Holstenstr
Beckstr
Marktstr

Chemnitzstr
Neuer
Pferdemarkt

Neuer Kamp   Feldstr
Feldstrasse

Kirchowstr
Thedestr
Holstenstr
Thadenstr
SCHANZENVIERTEL

Gilbertstr
Hein-Hoyer-Str
Amenstr
Budapester Str
HEILIGENGEISTFELD

Paul-Roosen-Str
Clemens-Schultz-Str
ST PAULI

Glacischausee

Grosse Freiheit
Talstr
Simon-von-Utrecht-Str
St Pauli

Louise-Schroeder-Str
Holstenstr
Nobistor
Seilerstr
Millerntorplatz
Elbpark

Königstr
Blücherstr
Reeperbahn
Reeperbahn
Spielbudenplatz

Hein
Köllisch
Platz
Hans-
Albers-Platz
Kastanienallee
Zirkusweg
Helgoländer Allee

Kirchenstr
Friedrichstr
Davidstr
Hopfenstr
Seewartenstr

Silbersackstwiete
Erichstr
Baldunstr
Bernhard-Nocht-Str
St-Pauli-Hafenstr

Breite Str
St-Pauli-Fischmarkt
Landungsbrücken

St Pauli Elbtunnel
St Pauli
Harbour

Elbe River

Sandthorhafen

E   F   G   H

Sights

Altonaer Balkon
VIEWPOINT

1 ⊙ MAP P126, C6

Thrill to some of Hamburg's best harbour views from this accurately named and quite pretty park. (Altona Balcony; off Klopstockstrasse; S Königstrasse)

Dockland
ARCHITECTURE

2 ⊙ MAP P126, B6

One of Hamburg's more striking waterfront structures and right on the water, Dockland was finished in 2006; it has wonderfully sharp angles and terrific views from the rooftop terrace. At first glance, it resembles a cruise ship moored at the docks. (Van-der-Smissen-Strasse 9; 112, S Königstrasse)

Worth a Trip: Barclaycard Arena

Hamburg's huge **Barclaycard Arena** (☑040-806 020 80; www.barclaycard-arena.de; Sylvesterallee 7; ⊙ticket office 11am-6pm Mon-Fri, 9am-2pm Sat, plus two hours before games) was extensively refurbished for the 2006 football World Cup, and is home to Bundesliga club Hamburger SV (www.hsv.de). Take S-Bahn 21 or 3 to 'Stellingen', which is linked by free shuttle buses to the stadium. For tickets, ring the ticket hotline, or visit the ticket office next to the E2 gate.

Rote Flora
CULTURAL CENTRE

3 ⊙ MAP P126, G1

One of the most outstanding remnants of the area's rougher days, the graffiti-covered Rote Flora looks one step away from demolition. Once the famous Flora Theatre, it's now an alternative cultural centre with a calendar of new music, protests and events. The city protected it from gentrification in 2014. (☑040-439 5413; www.roteflora.de; Schulterblatt 71; ⊙hours vary; S Sternschanze)

Altona Museum
MUSEUM

4 ⊙ MAP P126, C4

This moderately interesting collection is devoted to the art and culture of northern Germany since the 18th century. An unusual aspect is the focus on children's culture with a wonderful 'house of children's books'. We wouldn't cross town to see it, but it's worth an hour of your time if you're in the area. (☑040-428 1350; www.altonaermuseum.de; Museumsstrasse 23; adult/child €8.50/free; ⊙10am-5pm Mon & Wed-Fri, to 6pm Sat & Sun; S Altona)

Eating

In the village-like area around Altona train station, you'll find dozens of casual and ethnic eateries, especially in the gentrified climes of Ottensen to the west. These streets are among our favourite places for a meal in Hamburg.

The city's western riverfront, from Altona to Övelgönne, known

Rote Flora

as the Elbmeile (Elbe Mile), has a dense concentration of popular and trendy restaurants – many drawing menu inspiration from the waterfront location.

Tide
CAFE €

 5 MAP P126, A4

Part of the growing gourmet reputation of the Ottensen district of Altona, Tide is part cafe (sandwiches, soups, cakes and coffee) and part delicatessen (preserves made in-house from foraged berries, olive oils). Decorated with driftwood from Danish beaches, some of which are turned into artworks and for sale, Tide is filled with flavour and creativity. (☎040-4111 1499; www.tide.dk; Rothestrasse 53; mains from €5; ☺8am-6pm Mon-Fri, from 10am Sat & Sun; ⓢAltona)

Flying Market
VIETNAMESE €

6 MAP P126, A4

Vietnamese restaurants are all the rage in Hamburg, and this cool outpost is always popular for its fresh tastes and authentic Vietnamese cooking. Their soups (*phở*), noodle dishes and rice-noodle salads (*bun*) are the best we tasted in town. (☎040-8460 0904; Eulenstrasse 38; mains €8-12.50; ☺noon-10pm; ⓢAltona)

Eiscafe Eisliebe
ICE CREAM €

7 MAP P126, A4

Some of the yummiest ice cream you'll ever taste is scooped from this little hole in the wall (look for the queues). On any given day, you'll find around a dozen of its handmade, all-natural flavours.

Fresh berry creations are the stuff of fantasy. (📞040-3980 8482; Bei der Reitbahn 2; ice cream from €1.50; ⏱noon-9pm; ⑤Altona)

Mercado DELI €

8 MAP P126, B4

Forage for prime picnic fare (or eat in) at this market hall by Altona station. Stalls have everything from fresh Med fare to fine wines by the glass. But we also love the chance to see German *Hausfrauen* mingling with immigrants from across the world – this interaction is increasingly an Ottensen hallmark. (📞040-398 6840; www.mercado-hh.de; Ottenser Hauptstrasse 10; mains from €4.50; ⏱9am-8pm; ⑤Altona)

Super Mercato Italiano CAFE €

9 MAP P126, G1

The alt-vibe is perfectly contrasted by this very traditional Italian cafe and grocery, facing the inspirational near-ruin of the Rote Flora cultural centre. Any of three generations of owners will make you a perfect coffee, which you can enjoy on the wide pavement out front amidst a plethora of adjoining ethnic cafes. (📞040-434 114; www.super-mercato-italiano.net; Schulterblatt 82; snacks from €3; ⏱8am-6pm Mon-Sat; ⑤Sternschanze)

Bullerei INTERNATIONAL €€

10 MAP P126, G1

One of the coolest dining spaces in the city, Bullerei inhabits a con-

Klippkroog (p125)

LOOK DIE BILDAGENTUR DER FOTOGRAFEN GMBH/ALAMY ©

Worth a Trip: Blankenese

Once a former fishing village and haven for cutthroat pirates, Blankenese, 8km west of Altona, now boasts some of the finest and most expensive houses in Germany. For visitors, the area's attractiveness lies in its hillside labyrinth of narrow, cobbled streets, with a network of 58 stairways (4864 steps in total) connecting them. Begin along the waterfront by admiring the uber-luxurious villas, then take any of the lanes that lead inland.

To get here, take line S1 of the S-Bahn to Blankenese station. Blankenese lies within the inner-city ticket system and a single trip from the centre will cost €3.30 (although you're better off buying a day ticket for €6.40).

verted former slaughterhouse with lovely high ceilings and a real buzz that bounces off the walls – don't come here for a quiet romantic dinner. Service is cool and attentive, and the menu revolves around steak dishes and Italian-inflected choices. (☎040-3344 2110; www.bullerei.com; Lagerstrasse 34b; mains €10-25; ⏱11am-11pm; Ⓢ Sternschanze)

Altes Mädchen   EUROPEAN €€

11 ✖ MAP P126, H1

The lofty red-brick halls of a 19th-century animal market have been upcycled into a hip culinary destination that includes a coffee roastery, a celebrity chef restaurant, and this beguiling brewpub with a central bar, in-house bakery and garden. (☎040-800 077 750; www.altes-maedchen.com; Lagerstrasse 28b; mains €6-29; ⏱noon-late Mon-Sat, 10am-late Sun; Ⓢ Sternschanze, Ⓤ Sternschanze)

Von Der Motte   FAST FOOD €€

12 ✖ MAP P126, B4

In a tiny little pedestrian street, Von Der Motte does soups, sandwiches and salads – service is rapid, but the food slow-cooked and tasty. The breakfast menu is long, and the sandwiches are excellent. (☎040-8470 3618; www.vondermotte.de; Mottenburger Twiete 14; mains €8-12; ⏱10am-9pm Tue-Fri, to 6pm Sat & Sun; Ⓢ Altona)

Eisenstein   ITALIAN €€

13 ✖ MAP P126, A3

Altona's best pizza, in an artfully conceived space where the food is consistently good and the atmosphere clicks along nicely every night. It's hugely popular. The Sunday breakfast buffet (€21) is excellent. (☎040-390 4606; www.restaurant-eisenstein.de; Friedensallee 9; lunch mains from €7, pizza €9-15, 3-/4-course dinner set menu €34/39; ⏱noon-1am; Ⓢ Altona)

Altona's Street Festival: Altonale

Altona is a wonderful place to be in the first half of July when this street **festival** (www.altonale.de/altonale) runs for almost three weeks. Expect terrific food as well as live performances (including music, dance and theatre) and street art. There's a flea market on the final weekend.

Atlantik Fisch
SEAFOOD €€

14 🍴 MAP P126, D6

It doesn't get fresher than this Elbmeile gem. One of Hamburg's top seafood vendors has a simple cafe where top-notch dishes are served to thankful diners, sitting inside and out on wooden benches. The *Fischbrötchen* (fish sandwich) comes in 20 different varieties and is regularly voted among the best in the city. (📞040-391 123; www.atlantik-fisch.de; Grosse Elbstrasse 139; mains €8-18; ⏰6am-4pm Mon-Fri, from 7am Sat; 🚌112, 🚊Altona, Königstrasse)

Jools
CAFE €€

15 🍴 MAP P126, A5

Out in Altona's west, Jools is a terrific cafe-restaurant that does risotto, pasta, currywurst and even burgers. The tastes are fresh, the service is friendly, and the all-round feel here is fun and casual. (📞040-8812 8646; www.jools-hamburg.de; Bernadottestrasse 20; breakfast from €6, mains €8-14; ⏰10am-10pm Tue-Sat, to 7pm Sun; 🚊Altona)

Erikas Eck
GERMAN €€

16 🍴 MAP P126, H2

This pit-stop institution originally fed hungry workers from the nearby abattoir (today the central meat market) and now serves wallet-friendly but waist-expanding portions of schnitzel and other trad German fare to a motley crowd of clubbers, cabbies and cops. (📞040-433 545; www.erikas-eck.de; Sternstrasse 98; mains €8-13; ⏰5pm-2pm Mon-Fri, 5pm-9am Sat & Sun; 🚊Sternschanze)

Restaurant Kleinen Brunnenstrasse 1
EUROPEAN €€€

17 🍴 MAP P126, A4

The heart of northern Germany's slow food movement beats in this exquisite bistro. Menus change daily and *always* reflect what's in season and fresh. Preparations are simple, allowing flavours to shine. There's summer seating outside; book in advance. (📞040-3990 7772; www.kleine-brunnenstrasse.de; Kleinen Brunnenstrasse 1; mains lunch €12-23, dinner €18-26; ⏰noon-3pm & 6-10pm Mon-Fri, 6-10pm Sat & Sun; 🚊Altona)

Fischereihafen
SEAFOOD €€€

18 🍴 MAP P126, C6

Near the Elbmeile waterfront, Fischereihafen serves some of Hamburg's finest fish, including regional specialities, to a well-heeled clientele. No-frills outside, its 1st-floor, elegant maritime-themed dining room overlooks the Elbe. Lobster here comes in many forms. The Oyster Bar is a gentrified treat. (📞040-381 816; www.fischereihafenrestaurant.de; Grosse Elbstrasse 143; lunch mains €12-18, dinner mains €16-55; ⏰11.30am-10pm; 🚈Altona, Königstrasse)

Drinking

Good places to drink are an Altona trademark, but this is no Reeperbahn. Venues are smaller and more intimate here, and in the finest Altona tradition many double as cafes by day.

Katze
COCKTAIL BAR

19 🚇 MAP P126, G1

Small and sleek, this 'kitty' (*Katze* means cat) gets the crowd purring for well-priced cocktails (the best caipirinhas in town) and

great music (there's dancing on weekends). It's one of the most popular amongst the watering holes on this main Schanzenviertel booze strip. (📞040-5577 5910; Schulterblatt 88; ⏰1pm-3am Mon-Sat, to midnight Sun; 🚈Sternschanze)

Reh Bar
BAR

20 🚇 MAP P126, A4

If you could somehow bottle the Altona spirit and turn it into a bar, Reh Bar would come close. Cosy and welcoming, as good for a morning coffee as for a late-night cocktail, it draws a young crowd of local professionals every night. (📞040-3990 6363; Ottenser Hauptstrasse 52; ⏰10am-midnight Sun-Wed, to 2am Thu, to 4am Fri & Sat; 🚈Altona)

Fischereihafen

Familien-Eck

PUB

21  MAP P126, B3

Just a hole in the wall, but this Altona classic is everything a good Hamburg neighbourhood joint should be: friendly, unassuming, yet always ready for a laugh. Locals pop in, down a quick drink, joke, gossip and hurry on out. (☏040-9823 7896; www.familieneck.de; Friedensallee 2-4; ⏰3pm-5am; ☒Altona)

Café Knuth

CAFE

22 MAP P126, B4

Students, creative types and work colleagues come to chat in its split-level lounge areas. Or grab a picnic table outside and enjoy your drinks in the open air. Get here early and you can have breakfast. It's just as popular in the evening. (☏040-4600

8708; www.cafeknuth.com; Grosse Rainstrasse 21; ⏰9am-late; ☎; ⑤Altona)

Entertainment

Zeise Kino

CINEMA

23 MAP P126, A3

This excellent local arthouse cinema skips the mainstream films and shows them in their original version (ie with German subtitles) on Tuesdays. Otherwise, you'll need to speak German. You even get free popcorn. (☏040-3060 3682; www.zeise.de; Friedensallee 7-9; tickets €8; ⑤Altona)

Fabrik

LIVE PERFORMANCE

24 MAP P126, B3

They're making beautiful music in this former factory that's an iconic

Aurel (p125)

Altona venue, where the music ranges from classical to club and the program spans theatre to film. (☎040-391 070; www.fabrik.de; Barnerstrasse 36; ⓢAltona)

Shopping

The best shopping experiences are in the Altona streets west of the S-Bahn and train stations – here you'll find boutiques selling shoes, artworks and the full spectrum of homewares.

Wohnkultur 66   HOMEWARES

25 🄰 MAP P126, H2

What began as an obsession with world-renowned Danish furniture-maker Finn Juhl has turned into a more open love affair with Danish design in general. Many of these pieces are works of art and are priced accordingly, but the converted warehouse is the perfect setting for these perfect pieces. (☎040-436 002; www.wohnkultur66. de; Sternstrasse 66; ⊙noon-6pm Tue-Fri, to 4pm Sat; ⓊFeldstrasse)

Krupka   SHOES

26 🄰 MAP P126, A4

Stylish shoe heaven: rare brands of women's shoes plus Krupka's own designs are sold in this leather-scented shop. It's one of many alluring boutiques in the immediate area. (☎040-3990 3847;

Worth a Trip: Süllberg Hill

The best views of the Elbe (nearly 3km wide here) and its container ships are from the 75m-high **Süllberg Hill** (Süllbergweg). To get to Süllberg, take the S-Bahn to Blankenese, then bus 48 to Waseberg – having passed the beachfront restaurants and cafes – where you'll see a sign pointing to the nearby Süllberg. If you alight at the Krogers Treppe (Fischerhaus) bus stop, head up the Bornholdt Treppe and Süllbergweg. Or get off once the road starts winding and explore.

www.krupka-schuhe.de; Ottenser Hauptstrasse 55; ⊙10am-7pm Mon-Fri, to 5pm Sat; ⓢAltona)

Ply   HOMEWARES

27 🄰 MAP P126, B4

Furniture designs from the 1920s to 1960s, updated for a modern audience, make for a fascinating trip through German home design. There's so much you'll want to buy, with prices for the more modern pieces very reasonable. (☎040-2281 3330; www.ply.com; Kleine Rainstrasse 44; ⊙10am-7pm Mon-Fri, to 4pm Sat; ⓢAltona)

Survival Guide

Central transport hub Landungsbrücken IMAGEBROKER/ALAMY ©

Before You Go

Book Your Stay

Hamburg has excellent hotels, and standards are generally high across all budgets; even basic accommodation will likely be clean and comfortable. Reservations are a good idea between June and September, and around major public holidays and festivals. The city is big, and although it's easy to get from one area to another, consider where you'll be spending most of your time before you decide where to stay.

Accommodation Types

By German standards, Hamburg has a fairly standard variety of accommodation genres. These are the main ones:

Hotels Range from mom-and-pop joints to restored castles and international chains.

Hostels Both indie hostels and those belonging

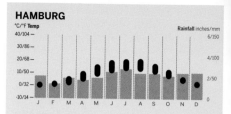

When to Go

o **Summer** (June to August) The busiest time, and the city has a real spring in its step; book ahead for most things.

o **Autumn** (September to November) Can be lovely, but cold.

o **Winter** (December to February) The cold means it's the quietest time to visit.

o **Spring** (March to May) Similar to autumn, chilly but sometimes delightful.

to Hostelling International are plentiful.

Pensionen The German version of B&Bs are prevalent in rural areas and good value.

Useful Websites

Bauernhof Urlaub (www.bauernhofurlaub. de) Farmstay central.

Bed and Breakfast (www.bed-and-break fast.de) Solid selection of B&Bs and private rentals.

Deutsches Jugend-herbergswerk (DJH; www.jugendherberge. de) Hostelling International-affiliated digs.

Germany Travel (www.germany.travel) Accommodation searchable by region and theme.

Independent Hostels of Germany (www. german-hostels.de) Wide range of indie hostels across the country.

Lonely Planet (www. lonelyplanet.com/ germany/hotels) Recommendations and bookings.

Best Budget

Generator Hostels (☏ 040-226 358 460; www.generatorhostels. com; Steintorplatz 3;

dm/d from €16/64; ☎; Ⓤ Hauptbahnhof-Süd) Modern rooms, great location and mix of dorms and doubles.

Instant Sleep Backpacker Hostel
(☎ 040-4318 2310; www.instantsleep.de; Max-Brauer-Allee 277; dm/s/d from €19/50/60; @ ☎; Ⓡ Sternschanze) Art on the walls, attractive rooms and great cafes nearby.

Jugendherberge Hamburg (☎ 040-570 1590; www.jugendherberge.de; Alfred-Wegener-Weg 5; dm €22-28, d/tr €79/99; ☎; Ⓢ & Ⓤ Landungsbrücken) Great views and a happening scene at this St Pauli youth hostel.

Meininger Hotel Hamburg City Center (☎ 040-2846 4388; www.meininger-hotels.com; Goetheallee 11; dm €15-30, s/d from €75/90; Ⓟ @ ☎; Ⓢ Altona) Hotel-hostel in wonderful Altona, with great facilities.

Alpha Hotel-Pension (☎ 040-245 365; www.alphahotel.biz; Koppel 4-6; s/d from €44/55; ➔ ☎; Ⓤ Hauptbahnhof-Nord) Friendly B&B in St Georg with rooftop corner.

Superbude St Georg (☎ 040-380 8780; www.superbude.de/hostel-hamburg/st-georg; Spaldingstrasse 152; r from €68; ☎) Fun hostel near St Georg with switched-on staff.

Best Midrange

Henri Hotel (☎ 040-554 357 557; www.henri-hotel.com; Bugenhagenstrasse 21; s/d from €98/118; ☎; Ⓢ Mönckebergstrasse) Retro design meets modern comforts in the heart of Altstadt.

Adina Apartment Hotel Speicherstadt (☎ 040-334 6080; www.adinahotels.com/hotel/hamburg-speicherstadt; Willy-Brandt-Strasse 25; r from €144; Ⓟ ✳ ☎ ✈; Ⓤ Messberg) Gorgeous modern studios with slick design and service.

Fritz im Pyjama Hotel (☎ 040-314 838; www.fritz-im-pyjama.de; Schanzenstrasse 101-103; s/d from €82/129; ☎; Ⓢ Sternschanze) Stylish boutique hotel with quirky decor in Schanzenviertel.

Hotel Motel One Hamburg Am Michel (☎ 040-3571 8900; www.motel-one.com; Ludwig-Erhard-Strasse 26; r from €79; ☎; Ⓤ St Pauli) High standards at a very reasonable price and has a cool vibe.

25hours Hotel HafenCity (☎ 040-257 7770; www.25hours-hotel.de; Überseeallee 5; r €100-225; Ⓟ ➔ ☎; Ⓤ Überseequartier) Very cool HafenCity address with stylish vintage and maritime decor.

Scandic Hamburg Emporio (☎ 040-432 1870; www.scandichotels.com; Dammtorwall 19; s/d from €139/149; ✳ @ ☎; Ⓤ Gänsemarkt) Excellent Scandinavian chain with fine rooms and good location.

Best Top End

Fairmont Vier Jahrseiten Hamburg (☎ 040-3494 3151; www.hvj.de; Neuer Jungfernstieg 9-14; r from €285; ✳ ☎ ✈; Ⓤ Stephansplatz) Hamburg's grandest old hotel with luxury rooms and water views.

Renaissance Hamburg Hotel (☎ 040-349 180; www.marriott.com; Grosse Bleichen; s/d from €159/179; ✳ ☎ ✈; Ⓢ & Ⓤ Jungfernstieg) Stunning hotel in the heart of Neustadt with a refined sensibility.

Hotel Atlantic

(📞 040-288 80; www. kempinski.com; An der Alster 72-79; s/d from €150/175; ❋ 🛜 🏊; Ⓤ Hauptbahnhof-Nord) Old-world charm close to the water in St Georg.

Hotel Wedina

(📞 040-280 8900; www.hotelwedina.de; Gurlittstrasse 23; r €125-275; Ⓟ @ 🛜; Ⓢ Hauptbahnhof) Intimate luxury St Georg hotel with literary atmosphere and celebrity guests.

Empire Riverside

(📞 040-311 190; www. empire-riverside.de; Bernhard-Nocht-Strasse 97; r €130-210, ste from €239; Ⓟ ❋ 🛜; Ⓤ St Pauli) Super-stylish modern outpost down overlooking the water in St Pauli.

The Madison Hotel

(📞 040-376 660; www.madisonhotel.de; Schaarsteinweg 4; s/d €159/179; ❋ @ 🛜; Ⓤ Baumwall) Superb location, superb rooms and personal service in Neustadt.

Arriving in Hamburg

Hamburg is well connected to the rest of Germany and further afield by extensive air, bus and train connections. Numerous airlines fly to Hamburg from around Europe, with some intercontinental flights as well. If you're travelling by train and bus, Hamburg is an important hub for northern Germany, with a number of long-distance domestic and international services, as well as shorter regional bus and train services. Flights, cars and tours can be booked online at lonelyplanet.com/bookings.

Hamburg Airport

Hamburg Airport

(Flughafen Hamburg Helmut Schmidt; HAM; 📞 040-507 50; www. hamburg-airport. de; Flughafenstrasse; Ⓡ Hamburg Airport) has frequent flights to domestic and European cities with Lufthansa

and most other major European carriers. Low-cost carriers include Ryanair, Air Berlin, easyJet and Eurowings. There are also a handful of intercontinental flights, such as to New York and Dubai.

Getting Around

Bicycle

Many hostels and some hotels arrange bike rental for guests. **Zweiradperle** (Map p46; 📞 040-3037 3474; www. zweiradperle.hamburg; Altstädter Strasse 3-7; rental per day from €14, tour incl rental from €25; ⏱10am-6pm daily Apr–mid-Oct, 11am-6pm Tue-Fri, to 3pm Sat mid-Oct–Mar, tour 10.30am daily; Ⓤ Steinstrasse) is also a good source.

StadtRad Hamburg (www.stadtradhamburg. de; 1st 30min free, then per min €0.08, per 24hr €12), run by Deutsche Bahn, operates from U-Bahn and S-Bahn stations and other key points across the city. Rentals are bright-red,

Hamburg Hauptbahnhof & Altona

Frequent trains serve regional and long-distance destinations from Hamburg. There are two mainline stations worth noting:

Hamburg Hauptbahnhof (Main Train Station; www.hamburger-hbf.de; Ⓡ Hauptbahnhof) The main rail hub for northern Germany. In addition to domestic services, there are several trains daily to Copenhagen (from €80, five to six hours).

Hamburg Altona (Ⓢ Altona) Many Hamburg trains, including some long-distance services, begin or end their journeys at this medium-sized station in the heart of its namesake neighbourhood.

Direct domestic services include:

DESTINATION	DURATION (HOURS)	COST
Berlin	1¾	from €30
Bremen	1	from €20
Cologne	4	from €36
Flensburg	2½	from €20
Frankfurt	3½	from €34
Kiel	1¼	from €20
Lübeck	¾	from €14.50
Munich	5¾-7	from €68
Schwerin	1	from €20
Stralsund	4-5	from €30

seven-gear bikes. You can register online or at the rental sites.

Bikes are allowed free of charge aboard S-/U-Bahn trains and buses outside peak hours (6am to 9am and 4pm to 6pm) and on ferries any time.

Car & Motorcycle

Driving around town is easy: thoroughfares are well signposted (watch for one-way streets in the city centre) and parking stations plentiful. Most inner-city parking stations charge around €4 per hour or €28 per day. Ask if your hotel has private or discounted parking when making your reservation.

For on-street parking, you'll need to pay between 9am and 8pm, and there's often a two-hour limit. It usually costs €0.50 per 10 minutes, or €6 for two hours.

Public Transport

HVV (☎ 040-194 49; www.hvv.de) operates buses, ferries, U-Bahn and S-Bahn and has several info centres, including at the Jun-

Tickets

The city is divided into zones. Ring A covers the city centre, inner suburbs and airport.

Day passes cover travel for one adult and up to three children aged six to 14. Kids under six travel free.

Train tickets must be purchased from machines at stations; bus tickets are available from the driver. Ticket types include the following:

TICKET GROSSBEREICH/RING A & B REGION	COST
Short journey/*Kurzstrecke* (only two to three stops)	€1.60
Single/*Einzelkarte*	€3.30
9-hour day pass/*9-Uhr-Tageskarte* (after 9am)	€6.40
Day pass/*Ganztageskarte* (valid from 6am to 6am the next day)	€7.70
Group day pass/*Gruppenkarte* (after 9am, up to five people of any age)	€12.00

If you catch a *Schnellbus* (express bus), it costs an extra €2.20.

Please note that there are no barriers at S-Bahn and U-Bahn stations. Random ticket checks are conducted on board.

gfernstieg S-/U-Bahn station and the Hauptbahnhof. Tickets start from €1.60.

Both bus and rail services run from 4am to midnight during the week and around the clock on weekends and the night before a public holiday; between approximately 12.30am and 4am Sunday to Thursday the night bus network takes over, converging on Rathausmarkt.

Bus

Public buses cover the city. Bus stops are well signposted and have route maps at each stop, but can be confusing unless you know where you're going.

There are three different types of buses:

MetroBus Around 25 different lines. They stop at all stops along a route.

SchnellBus Express buses with around 10 different routes; one useful express hop is between the Hauptbahnhof and Rathausmarkt (lines 35 and 37), with line 37 continuing on to St Pauli.

Nachtbus Night buses. Lines fan out across the city from Rathausmarkt once U-Bahn and S-Bahn trains have shut down for the night.

Ferry

The ferry system is an excellent way to get around, and a much cheaper alternative to the tourist-oriented harbour ferries. Ferries operate all along the Elbe and between HafenCity and Teufelsbrück.

Ferries run between 5.30am and 11.15pm; for most of that time, there are departures every 15 minutes.

Tickets are the same as those for bus and U-/S-Bahn services and can be purchased at vending machines at most stops.

Train

Easily the best way to get around the city, the U-Bahn (four lines) and S-Bahn (six lines) trains are easy to work out; maps of the system are found on all city maps and inside the stations.

There is little difference between the two types of service, although U-Bahn trains generally pass by more frequently (every two to 10 minutes) when compared to S-Bahn trains (every 10 to 20 minutes). U-Bahn and S-Bahn lines frequently intersect.

Taxi & Uber

Hamburg's cream-coloured taxis are easy to find – either flag down a passing taxi, catch one from a designated rank, or phone to have one pick you up. If doing the latter, **Taxi Hamburg** (☏040-666 666; www.taxihamburg.de) is one of the better companies.

Flagfall ranges between €3.50 and €4.20, depending on the time of day, with each kilometre charged at €1.50 to €2.50; the further you travel, the lower the per-kilometre tariff.

Uber (www.uber.com) is not widely used after a court ruled in May 2015 that traditional Uber services violated German transportation laws. Uber reacted by creating UberX, which uses only professionally licensed drivers. Trip costs tend to be between 3% and 12% less than regular taxi fares.

Essential Information

Accessible Travel

o Hamburg is fairly progressive when it comes to barrier-free travel. Access ramps and/or lifts are available in many public buildings, including train stations, museums, concert halls and cinemas.

o Trains, trams, underground trains and buses are increasingly accessible. Some stations also have grooved platform borders to assist blind passengers in navigating. Seeing-eye dogs are allowed on all forms of public transport. For the hearing impaired, upcoming station names are often displayed electronically on public transport.

o Newer hotels have lifts and rooms with extra-wide doors and spacious bathrooms. Some car-rental agencies offer hand-controlled vehicles and vans with wheelchair lifts at no charge, but you must reserve them well in advance. In parking lots and garages, look for designated spots marked with a wheelchair symbol.

Useful Resources

Download Lonely Planet's free Accessible Travel guides from http://lptravel.to/AccessibleTravel.

It's also worth checking out the online information

from Hamburg's city authorities (www.hamburg.com/visitors/hamburg-for/disabled-persons). It includes an accommodation list, deals with public transport and covers some of the city's barrier-free attractions.

Business Hours

The following are typical opening hours in Hamburg, although these may vary seasonally. Where hours vary across the year, we've provided those applicable in high season.

Banks 9am–4pm Monday to Friday, extended hours usually on Tuesday and Thursday, some open Saturday

Bars 6pm–1am

Cafes 8am–8pm

Clubs 11pm to late

Post offices 9am–6pm Monday to Friday, to 1pm Saturday

Restaurants 11am–11pm

Major stores and supermarkets 9.30am–8pm Monday to Saturday

Discount Cards

There are a handful of programs that allow you to cut costs while in Hamburg, although as always with such schemes you need to visit lots of places in a short time to make them worthwhile. Options include:

Hamburg Card (www.hamburg-travel.com/search-book/hamburg-card; 1 day €10.50) Offers discounts on entry to museums, theatre tickets and harbour tours, and free public transport (including harbour ferries). You'll need to plan well and read what's covered carefully to make it worthwhile. Purchase online or at any tourist office.

Hamburg City Pass (☏ 040-8788 098 50; www.turbopass.de; 1 day €39.90) Includes entry to most Hamburg museums and covers free public transport, a free harbour tour and free bus sightseeing. You'll need to keep moving to make it worthwhile, but it's generally a good deal. The pass can be bought online.

Kunstmeile Hamburg (Museum Mile; ☏ 040-428 134 110; www.kunstmeile-hamburg.de; 3-day pass adult/child €25/free, 1-year pass €36/free) Five of Hamburg's art museums offer a joint admission ticket that can provide great savings. Buy it at the museums. The standard version lasts for 12 months, but the cheaper three-day version is great value; the latter must be used over consecutive days.

Exchange Rates

Australia	A$1	€0.65
Canada	C$1	€0.65
Japan	¥100	€0.74
New Zealand	NZ$1	€0.60
UK	UK£1	€1.15
US	US$1	€0.81

For current exchange rates see www.xe.com.

Electricity

Type F
230V/50Hz

Type C
230V/50Hz

Emergency & Important Numbers

Germany's country code	☎ 49
International access code	☎ 00
Ambulance	☎ 112
Fire	☎ 110
Police	☎ 110

Money

Somewhat surprisingly, Germany remains largely a cash-based society and credit card use is not as common as you might think. International hotel chains, high-end restaurants, department stores and fancy boutiques usually accept credit cards, but enquire first, just to be on the safe side. ATMs are ubiquitous. Be wary of those not affiliated with major banks as they charge exorbitant transaction fees. ATMs do not recognise pins with more than four digits.

ATMs

o The easiest and quickest way to obtain cash is by using your debit (bank) card at a *Geldautomat* (ATM) linked to international networks such as Cirrus, Plus, Star and Maestro.

o ATM cards often double as debit cards, and many shops, hotels, restaurants and other businesses accept them for payment.

o Most cards use the 'chip and pin' system; instead of signing, you enter your PIN. If your card isn't chip-and-pin enabled, you may be able to sign the receipt, but ask first.

Cash

Cash is king in Hamburg. Always carry some with you and plan to pay cash almost everywhere. It's also a good idea to set aside a small amount of euros as an emergency stash.

The unit of currency in Germany is the euro (€). Euros come in seven notes (€5, €10, €20, €50, €100, €200 and €500) and eight coins (€0.01, €0.02, €0.05, €0.10, €0.20, €0.50, €1 and €2).

Changing Money

o Commercial banks usually charge a stiff fee (€5 to €10) per foreign-currency transaction, no matter the amount, if they offer exchange services at all.

o *Wechselstuben* (currency exchange offices) at airports, train stations and in bigger towns usually charge lower fees.

o Traveller-geared Reisebank (www.reisebank.de) branches are ubiquitous in Germany and are usually found at train stations. They keep longer hours than banks and are usually open on weekends.

Credit Cards

o Credit cards are becoming more widely accepted, but it's best not to assume you'll be able to use one – ask first. Sometimes, a minimum purchase amount applies.

o Visa and MasterCard are more commonly accepted than American Express or Diner's Club.

o Avoid getting cash advances on your credit card via ATMs, as fees are steep and you'll be charged interest immediately.

o Report lost or stolen cards to the central number ☎116 116 or the following: **American Express** ☎069-9797 1000; **MasterCard** ☎0800-819 1040; and **Visa** ☎0800-811 8440.

Tipping

Hotels €1 per bag is standard. It's also nice to leave a little cash for the room cleaners, say €1 or €2 per day.

Restaurants Restaurant bills always include *Bedienung* (service charge), but most people add 5% or 10% unless the service was truly abhorrent.

Bars About 5%, rounded to nearest euro. For table service, tip as for restaurants.

Taxis About 10%, rounded to the nearest euro.

Toilet attendants Loose change.

Public Holidays

Germany observes three secular and eight religious public holidays. Banks, shops, post offices and public services close on these days.

The following are *gesetzliche Feiertage* (public holidays):

Neujahrstag (New Year's Day) 1 January

Ostern (Easter) March/April; Good Friday, Easter Sunday and Easter Monday

Christi Himmelfahrt (Ascension Day) Forty days after Easter

Maifeiertag/Tag der Arbeit (Labour Day) 1 May

Pfingsten (Whit/Pentecost Sunday & Monday) Fifty days after Easter

Tag der Deutschen Einheit (Day of German Unity) 3 October

Weihnachtstag (Christmas Day) 25 December

Zweiter Weihnachtstag (Boxing Day) 26 December

Safe Travel

Hamburg is generally a safe city and most visitors visit without encountering any problems. That said, Hamburg is also undeniably sleazy in parts.

o Red-light districts are found around the Hauptbahnhof and the Reeperbahn.

○ Petty crime is rare but does occur in major tourist areas. Keep a careful eye on your belongings anywhere where there are crowds and large numbers of tourists.

○ In St Georg, Steindamm and Hansaplatz can be dicey, both day and night.

○ In areas where crime can be an issue, there's usually a strong police presence.

Toilets

○ German toilets are sit-down affairs. Men are expected to sit down when peeing.

○ Free-standing 24-hour self-cleaning toilet pods have become quite common. The cost is €0.50 and you have 15 minutes. Most are wheelchair-accessible.

○ Toilets in malls, clubs, beer gardens etc often have an attendant who expects a tip of between €0.20 and €0.50.

○ Toilets at the airport are free, but in larger train stations they are often maintained by private companies like McClean, which charge as much as €1.50 for the privilege.

Dos & Don'ts

Germany is a fairly formal society but in Hamburg you can generally get away with a little more. Even so, the following tips will help you avoid faux pas.

Greetings Shake hands and say *Guten Morgen* (before noon), *Guten Tag* (between noon and 6pm) or *Guten Abend* (after 6pm). Use the formal *Sie* (you) with strangers and only switch to the informal *du* and first names if invited to do so. With friends and children, use first names and *du*.

Asking for Help Germans use the same word – *Entschuldigung* – to say 'excuse me' (to attract attention) and 'sorry' (to apologise).

Eating & Drinking At the table, say *Guten Appetit* before digging in. Germans hold the fork in the left hand and the knife in the right hand. To signal that you have finished eating, lay your knife and fork parallel across your plate. If drinking wine, the proper toast is *Zum Wohl;* with beer it's *Prost*.

Tourist Information

Hamburg's tourist information offices are friendly and helpful, with a range of brochures on offer. Ask for the monthly *Hamburg Guide*, which is not always on display. Useful offices include:

Tourist Information Hauptbahnhof (☎ 040-3005 1701; www.hamburg-travel. com; Hauptbahnhof, near Kirchenallee exit; ⏰9am-7pm Mon-Sat, 10am-6pm Sun; ☒Hauptbahnhof, Ⓤ Hauptbahnhof) Busy all the time and with plenty of brochures and booking information.

Tourist Information Airport (Terminals 1 & 2; ⏰6am-11pm) On the arrivals level, next to the baggage collection belts.

Tourist Information am Hafen (☎ 040-3005 1701; www.hamburg-travel. com; btwn piers 4 & 5, St Pauli Landungsbrücken; ⏰9am-6pm Sun-Wed, to 7pm Thu-Sat; Ⓢ Landungsbrücken) No hotel bookings.

Visas

Germany is one of 26 member countries of the Schengen Convention, under which 22 EU countries (all but Bulgaria, Cyprus, Ireland, Romania and the UK) plus Iceland, Norway, Liechtenstein and Switzerland have abolished checks at common borders.

The visa situation for entering Germany is as follows:

Citizens or residents of EU & Schengen countries No visa required.

Citizens or residents of Australia, Canada, Israel, Japan, New Zealand & the USA No visa required for tourist visits of up to 90 days out of every 180 days.

Other countries Check with a German embassy or consulate.

To work or study in Germany A special visa may be required – contact a German embassy or consulate before travel.

Language

It's easy to pronounce German because almost all sounds are also found in English – just read our pronunciation guides as if they were English and you'll be understood.

In German, word stress falls mostly on the first syllable – in our pronunciation guides the stressed syllable is indicated with italics.

Note that German has polite and informal forms for 'you' (*Sie* and *du* respectively). When addressing people you don't know well, use the polite form. In this language guide, polite forms are used, unless you see (pol/inf) which indicates we've given both options. Also note that (m/f) indicates masculine and feminine forms.

To enhance your trip with a phrasebook, visit **lonelyplanet.com**.

Basics

Hello.
Guten Tag. — goo·ten taak

Goodbye.
Auf — owf
Wiedersehen. — vee·der·zey·en

How are you? (pol/inf)
Wie geht es — vee gayt es
Ihnen/dir? — ee·nen/deer

Fine, thanks.
Danke, gut. — dang·ke goot

Please.
Bitte. — bi·te

Thank you.
Danke. — dang·ke

Excuse me.
Entschuldigung. — ent·shul·di·gung

Sorry.
Entschuldigung. — ent·shul·di·gung

Yes./No.
Ja./Nein. — yah/nain

Do you speak (English)?
Sprechen Sie — shpre·khen zee
Englisch? — eng·lish

I (don't) understand.
Ich verstehe — ikh fer·shtay·e
(nicht). — (nikht)

Eating & Drinking

I'm a vegetarian. (m/f)
Ich bin Vegetarier/ — ikh bin ve·ge·
Vegetarierin. — tah·ri·er/
— ve·ge·tah·ri·e·in

Cheers!
Prost! — prawst

That was delicious!
Das war sehr — das vahr zair
lecker! — le·ker

Please bring the bill.
Die Rechnung, — dee rekh·nung
bitte. — bi·te

I'd like ...
Ich möchte ... — ikh merkh·te ...

a coffee	*einen Kaffee*	ai·nen ka·fay
a glass of wine	*ein Glas Wein*	ain glas wain
a table for two	*einen Tisch für zwei Personen*	ai·nen tish für tsvai per·zaw·nen
two beers	*zwei Bier*	tsvai beer

Key Words

bar (pub)	*Kneipe*	knai·pe
bottle	*Flasche*	fla·she
bowl	*Schüssel*	shü·sel
bread	*Brot*	brawt
breakfast	*Frühstück*	frü·shtük

butter	*Butter*	*bu*·ter
cheese	*Käse*	*kay*·ze
cold	*kalt*	kalt
cup	*Tasse*	*ta*·se
daily special		
Gericht des Tages	ge·*rikht* des *tah*·ges	
delicatessen		
Feinkost-geschäft	*fain*·kost ge·sheft	
desserts		
Nachspeisen	*nahkh*·shpai·zen	
dinner		
Abendessen	*ah*·bent·e·sen	
drink list		
Getränke-karte	ge·*treng*·ke kar·te	
egg/eggs	*Ei/Eier*	ai/*ai*·er
fork	*Gabel*	*gah*·bel
glass	*Glas*	glahs
grocery store		
Lebensmittel-laden	*lay*·bens·mi·tel lah·den	
hot (warm)	*warm*	varm
knife	*Messer*	*me*·ser
lunch		
Mittagessen	*mi*·tahk·e·sen	
market	*Markt*	markt

pepper	*Pfeffer*	*pfe*·fer
plate	*Teller*	*te*·ler
restaurant		
Restaurant	res·to·*rahng*	
salt	*Salz*	zalts
set menu	*Menü*	may·*nü*
spicy	*würzig*	*vür*·tsikh
spoon	*Löffel*	*ler*·fel
sugar	*Zucker*	*tsu*·ker
with	*mit*	mit
without	*ohne*	*aw*·ne

Shopping

I'd like to buy ...
Ich möchte ... kaufen. ikh *merkh*·te ... *kow*·fen.

May I look at it?
Können Sie es mir zeigen? *ker*·nen zee es meer *tsai*·gen

How much is it?
Wie viel kostet das? vee feel *kos*·tet das

That's too expensive.
Das ist zu teuer. das ist tsoo *toy*·er

Can you lower the price?
Können Sie mit dem Preis heruntergehen? *ker*·nen zee mit dem prais he·*run*·ter·gay·en

There's a mistake in the bill.
Da ist ein Fehler in der Rechnung. dah ist ain *fay*·ler in dair *rekh*·nung

Emergencies

Help!
Hilfe! *hil*·fe

Call a doctor!
Rufen Sie einen Arzt! *roo*·fen zee *ai*·nen artst

Call the police!
Rufen Sie die Polizei! *roo*·fen zee dee po·li·*tsai*

Question Words

How?	*Wie?*	vee
What?	*Was?*	vas
When?	*Wann?*	van
Where?	*Wo?*	vaw
Who?	*Wer?*	vair
Why?	*Warum?*	va·*rum*

I'm lost.
Ich habe — ikh *hah*·be
mich verirrt. — mikh fer·*irt*

I'm ill.
Ich bin krank. — ikh bin krangk

Where's the toilet?
Wo ist die Toilette? — vo ist dee to·a·*le*·te

Time

What time is it?
Wie spät ist es? — vee shpayt ist es

It's (10) o'clock.
Es ist (zehn) Uhr. — es ist (tsayn) oor

morning	*Morgen*	*mor*·gen
afternoon	*Nach-mittag*	*nahkh*·mi·tahk
evening	*Abend*	*ah*·bent
yesterday	*gestern*	*ges*·tern
today	*heute*	*hoy*·te
tomorrow	*morgen*	*mor*·gen

Days

Monday	*Montag*	*mawn*·tahk
Tuesday	*Dienstag*	*deens*·tahk
Wednesday	*Mittwoch*	*mit*·vokh
Thursday	*Donnerstag*	do·ners·tahk
Friday	*Freitag*	*frai*·tahk
Saturday	*Samstag*	*zams*·tahk
Sunday	*Sonntag*	*zon*·tahk

Months

January	*Januar*	*yan*·u·ahr
February	*Februar*	*fay*·bru·ahr
March	*März*	merts
April	*April*	a·*pril*
May	*Mai*	mai
June	*Juni*	*yoo*·ni
July	*Juli*	*yoo*·li
August	*August*	ow·*gust*
September	*September*	zep·*tem*·ber
October	*Oktober*	ok·*taw*·ber
November	*November*	no·*vem*·ber
December	*Dezember*	de·*tsem*·ber

Numbers

1	*eins*	ains
2	*zwei*	tsvai
3	*drei*	drai
4	*vier*	feer
5	*fünf*	fünf
6	*sechs*	zeks
7	*sieben*	*zee*·ben
8	*acht*	akht
9	*neun*	noyn
10	*zehn*	tsayn
100	*hundert*	*hun*·dert
1000	*tausend*	*tow*·sent

Transport & Directions

Where's ...?
Wo ist ...? — vaw ist ...

What's the address?
Wie ist die — vee ist dee
Adresse? — a·*dre*·se

Can you show me (on the map)?
Können Sie es mir — *ker*·nen zee es meer
(auf der Karte) — (owf dair *kar*·te)
zeigen? — *tsai*·gen

I want to go to ...
Ich mochte — ikh *merkh*·te
nach ... fahren. — nahkh ... *fah*·ren

What time does it leave?
Wann fährt es ab? — van fairt es ap

What time does it arrive?
Wann kommt   van komt
es an?   es an

Does it stop at ...?
Hält es in ...?   helt es in ...

I want to get off here.
Ich mochte hier   ikh *merkh*·te heer
aussteigen.   ows·*shtai*·gen

boat	*Boot*	bawt
bus	*Bus*	bus
metro	*U-Bahn*	oo·bahn
plane	*Flugzeug*	flook·tsoyk
train	*Zug*	tsook

Accommodation

campsite
Campingplatz   kem·ping·plats

guesthouse
Pension   pahng·*zyawn*

hotel
Hotel   ho·*tel*

inn
Gasthof   gast·hawf

room in a private home
Privatzimmer   pri·*vaht* tsi·mer

youth hostel
Jugend-   yoo·gent·
herber·ge   herber ge

Do you have *Haben Sie*   hah·ben
a ... room? *ein ...?*   zee ain?

   double
   Doppelzimmer   do·pel·
     tsi·mer

   single
   Einzelzimmer   ain·tsel·
     tsi·mer

How much *Wie viel*   vee feel
is it per ...? *kostet*   kos·tet
   es pro...?   es praw?

   night *Nacht*   nakht

   person *Person*   per·
     zawn

Is breakfast included?
Ist das Frühstück   ist das *frü*·shtük
inklusive?   in·kloo·zee·ve

Behind the Scenes

Send Us Your Feedback

We love to hear from travellers – your comments help make our books better. We read every word, and we guarantee that your feedback goes straight to the authors. Visit **lonelyplanet.com/contact** to submit your updates and suggestions.

Note: We may edit, reproduce and incorporate your comments in Lonely Planet products such as guidebooks, websites and digital products, so let us know if you don't want your comments reproduced or your name acknowledged. For a copy of our privacy policy visit lonelyplanet.com/privacy.

Anthony's Thanks

I was greeted warmly wherever I went in Hamburg – there are too many people to thank them all individually. Special thanks to Thomas, Heike and Anouk Süssenbach. At Lonely Planet, I am grateful to my editor Niamh O'Brien for sending me to such wonderful places. Thanks to Ron and Elaine Pumpa for such inspiration. And to my family – Marina, Carlota, Valentina and Jan: *con todo mi amor*.

Acknowledgements

Cover photograph: Warehouse in Speicherstadt, reach-art/Getty Images©

Photographs pp32-3 (clockwise from top left): Bildagentur-online/Joko/Alamy©; Nik Waller Productions/Shutterstock©; Bildagentur-online/Joko/Alamy©

This Book

This 1st edition of Lonely Planet's *Pocket Hamburg* guidebook was researched and written by Anthony Ham. This guidebook was produced by the following:

Destination Editor
Niamh O'Brien

Senior Product Editor
Genna Patterson

Product Editor Kate Kiely

Senior Cartographer
Valentina Kremenchutskaya

Book Designer
Clara Monitto

Assisting Editors
Samantha Forge, Ross Taylor

Cover Researcher
Naomi Parker

Thanks to Janet Austin, Hannah Cartmel, Andrea Dobbin, Mark Griffiths, Anne Mason, Martine Power

Index

See also separate subindexes for:

⊗ **Eating p156**

◉ **Drinking p157**

✪ **Entertainment p157**

◉ **Shopping p157**

Sights 000

Map Pages 000

🔒 Shopping

Our Writer

Anthony Ham

Anthony has been travelling the world in search of stories for more than two decades. Studying German at university began a life-long love affair with a country to which he returns whenever he can. He has written more than 120 guidebooks for Lonely Planet, including destinations across Europe, Africa, the Middle East and Australia, and he writes for magazines and newspapers around the world.

Published by Lonely Planet Global Limited
CRN 554153
1st edition – Mar 2019
ISBN 978 1 78701 775 7
© Lonely Planet 2019   Photographs © as indicated 2019
10 9 8 7 6 5 4 3 2 1
Printed in Singapore